Nobody
Believed Me

To

Marie and Janet,

Lovely to meet you,

Best wishes

Lesley Newman

xx.

Nobody
Believed Me

*A harrowing true story
of abuse survival*

Lesley Newman

THE CHOIR PRESS

First published in the United Kingdom in 2018 by
The Choir Press

ISBN 978-1-911589-91-4

Dedication

This book is dedicated to my best friend Margo Tevendale. Without her support and encouragement I may never have survived long enough to write it.

Foreword

———◦⟨⟨⟩⟩◦———

Isit waiting for the anaesthetist to come and fetch me for my cancer operation. I don't think I have any chance of escape, dressed in a hospital gown, wearing anti-clot stockings and red slipper socks. I guess it wouldn't take too long to find me! I have sent my husband away to get some breakfast and take himself home, pending the outcome of my operation. But what will that be? Am I going to die on the operating table? Will I live but find the cancer has spread? This silent killer is almost as emotionally testing as the silent secret I have kept hidden from most people for nearly fifty years. I still feel a sense of shame and embarrassment when anyone asks about my childhood. I have no idea why I feel like this – what happened was not my fault.

I read the book I have brought in with me, a hefty novel with much to contemplate about who the villain might be. I say a prayer. Not usually one for praying, I decide that I will put the Almighty to the test and see if he exists, and if he does, will he hear my prayer and will he help me in my hour of need?

I am the last patient on the operating list for today. I pray that the surgeon will not be in a bad mood because his last patient has died on the table. I hope that those involved with my operation will be suitably fed and watered, so that I have a fighting chance of having a proper job done with no errors due to hunger or fatigue. It's funny how you think of these things when your life is in someone else's hands.

My mind goes back to the thing that has been eating

away at me for years: the trauma I suffered as a child. Adopted and abused for many years through the 1960s and 70s, I always wanted someone to believe me, but nobody ever did. If I died on the operating table, there would be nobody to tell my story, because nobody actually knows my story. I have kept my past life and eleven years of physical and emotional abuse a secret from friends and colleagues for all these years. There is nobody to vindicate me, so I must do it for myself. I vow that if I live through this, the world will finally know what happened to me.

This is my story, told in my words. The story of a child-hood cruelly stolen from me by my abusers, the people who adopted me to give me a better life. A story that is searingly painful but true. I hope by reading this book, you will become more aware of the issues surrounding the abhorrent abuse of children and you will see the world around you through different eyes. Abuse happens in all sorts of homes, be they rich or poor. Abuse, like cancer, does not discriminate. It could happen next door to you and you would never know. Abusers are very clever and keep their tracks well covered, lest they be exposed.

People have asked me why I have not written this book in the first person. The answer is simple. I couldn't; it remains too painful, even now. Writing in the third person allowed my mind the freedom to recall, without fear, the dreadful abuse I endured.

Writing this book and exposing the abuse I suffered and those who abused me has given me the inner peace I have sought for many years. No amount of counselling or pills helped to erase the memories. Instead I chose to write down the details of the abuse I suffered, in the hope that others may know that they must never feel alone in their silent suffering.

Chapter 1

The Journey Begins

———•❧•———

Reading wasn't a big town in the 1950s. The university was the most imposing building in the area, apart from the Huntley & Palmers biscuit factory. Lesley's house was on Peppard Road, on the corner opposite the university. It was tiny – in fact, it was a bit too small for the family of four who lived there. It was more like a cottage. There was a very small living room, which also served as a dining room. The square dining table stood in the corner of the room, with four chairs around it. There wasn't much room left for any other furniture. Two easy chairs were crammed in against the wall, inches from the dinner table. A valve radio stood on the floor in the corner. There was a tiny kitchenette and a downstairs bathroom. A narrow staircase led up to two very small bedrooms. The two girls shared a room. Lesley, being the older of the two, had a single bed, while her baby sister Karen slept in a cot opposite her. Their parents had the slightly larger room at the front. Lesley and Karen had no room to play in their bedroom. The rooms were so small that all the clothes were kept in boxes underneath the beds.

The electric was unreliable and many a night time trip to the toilet had to be made in complete darkness. Lesley had a pot under her bed which served as her toilet overnight, should the need arise. There was no front garden, just a small patch of gravel which led straight out on to the road. Luckily, being opposite the university, the road was always quiet. At the back was an enclosed yard, far too small for two children to play in, and besides, it housed the dustbin and a few neighbourhood rats. The children spent most of their lives indoors, unless they were taken out by their parents or grandparents.

Raymond was a laboratory technician at the university. The laboratories were directly opposite the house, so he was able to come home every lunchtime to join his family for a bite to eat before returning for the afternoon. Sometimes Raymond would take his daughters to the laboratory, where he did tests on animals. Too young to really understand, Lesley was fascinated with the rows and rows of cages of rats, mice, chickens and rabbits. She thought they were pets for the university staff and her father was very careful not to tell her the truth. Raymond was a tall man, with thinning dark hair and a moustache. He had been in the RAF and liked to think of himself as a suitable husband and father for his wife and children.

His wife Mary was a beauty, with beautiful big dark brown eyes and shiny long black hair. She was medium height, very slim and always immaculately dressed, sporting bright red lipstick, even when she just went to the local shop for milk! Mary struggled to be a good housewife and mother. She had worked as a secretary prior to having her children, and she found the endless round of nappy changes and feeds extremely tedious. She missed the everyday office routine and being able to dress up like she used to. She felt trapped in this tiny house and often vented her frustrations on her husband when he returned home at night.

To make matters worse, Raymond's parents were less than happy about the marriage and refused to have anything to do with Mary or their two granddaughters.

Mary was of Iranian stock and her parents were staunch members of the Baha'i faith, a weird and wonderful religious cult that professed itself to be the religion for the modern age. The Iranian side of the family expected Mary to be a good housewife and produce children, which she rebelled against on a daily basis. On the other hand, Raymond's parents belonged to the Salvation Army and could not understand why their son had chosen to marry a foreigner at all. This was the 1950s, when marriage between different races or religions was frowned upon. Raymond felt torn between his parents and his in-laws.

Raymond and Mary did their best for their two small daughters, Lesley, who was three, and her sister Karen, who was two. Before Karen was born, Mary had delivered of a boy, but the child was stillborn. She took the loss of her baby very badly and vented her anger and grief on her husband. They felt that having another child immediately would make things better, but unfortunately it had the opposite effect. Mary had hoped to give birth to a boy again, so when Karen was born she did not bond with the baby and started to display extreme cruelty towards the child.

Lesley was a bright little girl with dark hair and big brown eyes to match. She was an affectionate child and loved her little sister. Karen was a fragile child. She had beautiful jet-black curly hair, just like her mother, but she was delicate, and Lesley thought she cried too much. Lesley would discover much later on in her life that her mother had tried to drown her baby sister in a bath full of boiling water. The poor baby was badly scalded and that was why Karen was so fragile and always crying. This shocked Lesley, who had always believed her mum to be a gentle, if flawed, person.

3

Lesley aged three, before the adoption.

Raymond was not having a very easy time. He was trying desperately to find a larger property so that he could provide a better home for his wife and children. He hoped that by doing this he would win over his in-laws, who had never considered him an appropriate husband for their daughter. He tried several times to negotiate a truce with his own parents, but their strict Salvation Army rules meant that they would never allow things to change. On top of this, Raymond was not a member of the Baha'i faith, a fact that was frowned upon by the elders of the religion in Reading. He made the difficult decision to go against his parents and become a member of this strange faith, which only served to seal what would become a permanent rift in the family. Raymond tried his hardest to appease his high-maintenance wife who always expected money to buy makeup, perfume, new clothes or shoes for herself and her daughters. Raymond's salary was not a large one and, despite his best efforts at negotiation, the bank refused to lend him any more money for a larger mortgage. Raymond was totally unaware that a situation was developing in Peppard Road, brought about by his wife. A few of the neighbours had been spreading rumours that Mary was being seen out every afternoon, without her two young daughters. Knowing that Raymond was at work, the neighbours waited till he returned home in the evening and expressed their concerns to him. He questioned Mary about this, but she said that the neighbours must have imagined it, swearing she had been at home all afternoon. However, her lies did not convince the neighbours and they eventually reported the matter to the local authority. When the council officers came to visit, Mary said that she must have been in the back yard and not heard them knocking at the door. The visiting officers remained totally unconvinced by this story and repeatedly visited the property, only to be told in no uncertain terms by Mary to go away and leave her family alone. The whole situation soon spiralled out of control and the lives of these two little girls were torn apart forever.

What follows is the story of Lesley's life from 1961 to 1974.

Chapter 2

Life Changes Forever

---◦◦◦◦---

'Now then, darlings, Mummy has to go out for a while, so you will both need to hide again.' Lesley could never understand why their mother would never take her or her sister into town with her in the afternoons.

'But Mummy,' she protested, 'why can't we go with you? I wanted to get some of those nice sweeties in that special shop Daddy takes us to.'

'Not today, dear,' her mother continued.

Lesley was a bit upset by this. Her father always used to take the girls to a certain shop in town where the nice lady would give them a free strawberry split ice cream. The girls looked forward to these trips with their father. They had to cross the railway line using a rickety bridge and quite often as they crossed a steam engine would roar past underneath and the two little girls would shriek with fear, hands over their ears as the train raced past, blowing its whistle and engulfing them in a thick cloud of white smoke as it sped past en route to the West Country.

'Now, come along,' Lesley's mum continued. 'You and your sister need to hide in your special cupboard, like you always do. You must try and keep your sister quiet, in case the bad people come.' Mary's voice was showing signs of irritation now. Lesley didn't like the bad people. They always seemed to come when her mother was out. They would bang on the door and shout through the letterbox. The girls found it very frightening. They were convinced that one day the bad people would come in and take them both away. It was strange – they never came when Mummy was there.

Lesley was never allowed to tell her daddy about what was happening while he was at work. Mary convinced her that Daddy was much too tired after work to listen to tales about what had happened during the day, so Raymond never actually got to know what was going on under his roof in his absence. It was dark in the cupboard and their mother wouldn't let them have a light, as she said it might fall over and cause a fire and they would both die. Lesley didn't like that idea, but she didn't much like the cupboard either. The only light in there was through the gap at the top of the door. Later on in life, both girls would be terrified of total darkness.

'Alright, Mummy,' Lesley said. 'Come on, Karen, let's go to the cupboard again. You take your teddy and I will take my favourite dolly, Yvonne. Oh, hang on, Mummy, I had better go to the toilet before you go out, in case I need to go before you get home.' Lesley went to the toilet and gathered her dolly up into her arms. She ushered her sister into the dark cupboard and wished they didn't have to keep doing this. It just didn't make sense to this little three-year-old that they were never taken out to town, only when Daddy took them.

The girls knew this cupboard very well. They had spent many hours in there over the previous months. They scrambled in and their mother locked the door from the outside. Lesley tried not to worry, but something in her little mind told her that this was not how things were meant to be. 'Don't be too long, Mummy,' Lesley said. Karen started to cry. She had been locked in the cupboard many times before with her older sister, but that didn't mean she didn't find it terrifying. Lesley cuddled her and reassured her that their mother would soon return. Lesley also remembered what Mary had said about the bad people, so she did her best to keep her sister calm and quiet.

It was whilst Mary was out on one of her endless shopping trips that the bad people came. They knocked at the door and hammered on the window, calling for the children and for Mary. The two girls clung to each other, frightened.

'It's okay,' Lesley whispered. 'They'll go away in a minute when nobody answers the door.'

'But what if they get in and take us away? I'm frightened!' Karen wailed.

'Sshh,' said Lesley, clamping her hand over the toddler's mouth. 'Mummy said we have to be quiet. Shut up. Shut up!'

Like a frightened rabbit, Karen scrambled to the corner of the cupboard, sulking. After a few minutes the knocking stopped and the two girls forgot their terror. They began to play with their toys and squabble as sisters do. Soon, Mary returned from her shopping trip with new dresses and sweets for her daughters.

The memory of being shut in that cupboard would remain with Lesley for the rest of her life.

Little did these two innocent young girls realise just how much their lives would change. In the next few months, they would be torn away from their parents and grand-parents. Their lives were about to be ripped apart, they would be separated from each other and their relatives, and it would be many years before they would be reunited.

The girls both adored their grandparents, Banoo and Rustom. They were a very sweet Iranian couple, staunch members of the Baha'i faith. Mary had explained to the girls that they were her parents. Unlike Raymond's parents, who refused to see their grandchildren, Banoo and Rustom adored the girls and would spend much of their time with them. Both in their mid-fifties, they lived a quiet life in another part of Reading.

Neither grandparent was very tall. Rustom's hair was starting to go grey, but it gave him a distinguished look. He had worked for multi-national companies previously but had taken early retirement and decided on a change of career to see out his working life and was now in insurance. His wife Banoo was a plump lady who, like her husband, had greying hair, but streaked with wisps of white. She was a very gentle lady, softly spoken and always jolly.

Rustom had a funny little car with two wheels at the front and one at the back. The girls loved sitting in there, hanging on as their granddad went round a bend or over a bump. The car bounced up and down and the girls would shriek with glee as their heads hit the roof of the car. Many years later, Lesley would see one of these cars, called a Messerschmitt, at a vintage show and shed a tear as many fond memories of those days flooded back.

Banoo and Rustom were very well thought of in the Baha'i faith and wanted to ensure that the girls were brought up in this religion. They would try and teach them little prayers to say. Raymond was not too happy with this. He wanted them to be able to make their own choice when they were older. He found it difficult that his in-laws always seemed to force their views upon his children.

One day, in May 1961, Banoo and Rustom arrived to collect their grandchildren. They seemed to be in a great hurry to get the girls out of the house, but Lesley and

Karen weren't worried as they adored their grandparents and didn't mind at all. To them, this was just going to be another fun-packed afternoon at Grandma and Granddad's house, but it was going to take a sinister turn later on that day.

As it got closer to their bedtime, the girls were getting tired and began to squabble and fight over their toys.

'You'll have to behave better than that when you get home,' Banoo said. 'Your daddy is not at all well and Mummy will be upset.'

The girls looked puzzled. 'Daddy was fine when we saw him this morning,' Lesley said cheekily. After all, in their little minds, their parents were never ill!

'I know, dear,' Banoo said, 'but sometimes people get poorly very quickly. Your daddy has a bad tummy and the nurses and doctors at the hospital are trying to make him better.' Lesley would remember those words for many years, until the real and awful truth emerged, when she was very much older.

The two girls sat in Rustom's new car, quietly thinking about their father. Their granddad had recently joined an insurance company as a salesman. He needed a bigger, more reliable car for his job, visiting clients in their homes to sell them insurance policies. His new green minivan was far more comfortable than the funny little bubble car and the girls didn't hit their heads on the roof when it bounced on the road. Granddad was very proud of his new purchase and the girls were not allowed to climb all over the seats as they had done in the bubble car.

'Granddad,' said Lesley.

'What is it, dear?' Granddad asked.

'Why is Daddy's tummy poorly?'

Rustom thought for a moment. He adored these two

mischievous little girls, his only grandchildren. He had to be careful how he answered this question, he didn't want to frighten or alarm the children. He decided to play it safe. 'Well, you see, your dad had a sandwich at lunchtime. Something in the sandwich made his tummy ache very badly, so he had to go to hospital. Don't worry – they'll soon make him better.' Rustom was hoping and praying that the girls wouldn't ask any more questions. He didn't like lying to them, but he needed to protect them from the awful truth.

By the time the girls arrived back at their tiny house, they were tired, but worried about their father. They clambered out of Rustom's car, falling over each other to race inside and ask their mother how he was.

'Careful!' Rustom said. 'You'll trip up in a minute and break something!'

The girls raced indoors but the sight that met them in the living room was not what they had expected. Mary was sitting on the floor, sobbing uncontrollably. She was holding Raymond's laboratory jacket in her arms and screaming, 'Why? Why? Why?' over and over again. Karen started to cry, then Lesley started crying too. They had no understanding of the scene before them. Lesley put her arms on her mother's shoulder. 'Why are you crying, Mummy?' she asked. 'Granddad said Daddy has a bad tummy ache and the hospital are trying to make him better.'

Mary threw her head back and looked over at Rustom, who was helplessly watching from the doorway. 'I ... I ... I didn't know what to tell them,' he said.

Mary looked at her two daughters, who were now crying at her feet. 'I'm sad, my darlings,' she said. 'You see, your daddy has died. He won't be coming back.' The two girls looked at their mother, terror in their little faces, then they looked at their granddad, who rushed forward to put his arms round them. Both children started to scream, Karen didn't know why Lesley was screaming but she screamed anyway.

Mary stood up. She said to Rustom, 'Please can you take the children for tonight? I really can't cope with them at the moment.'

Rustom put his arms round the girls and guided them to the door. 'Come on, you two,' he said. 'You can come and stay with us till your mum feels better.'

The two forlorn little figures held hands and clambered into Granddad's van. They were not aware that this would be the end of family life as they knew it. On the way to their grandparents' house, Lesley tried to make sense of what was going on. At three, she was an intelligent, knowing little girl, and something wasn't right about this situation. She wondered whether her mother had killed her father during one of the terrible rows they seemed to have every night. Why did her father have a bad stomach? Had their mother killed him with a knife? Lesley's little mind was working overtime but she decided she must be strong for her little sister, who had no idea what all the fuss was about. It was the 31st of May 1961.

*

The girls were now living with Banoo and Rustom full-time. Mary's visits to her children decreased significantly within a very short space of time. In fact, in no time at all she had abandoned her children and never spent any time with them again. The children could not understand what had happened. Lesley had seen a dead rat and a dead squirrel in the yard at the back of their house in Peppard Road, so she knew that death was quite a serious thing.

Any questions about their dad were met with a wall of silence. The children did not attend their father's funeral. To this day, neither daughter knows when the funeral was or who attended.

The girls soon got used to Mary not being around. They loved being with Banoo and Rustom. Their house was much bigger than the house in Peppard Road and it had a much bigger garden, so the girls could play outside safely. There were trees to climb and Rustom bought them a ball to throw around the garden. The girls played hide and seek indoors and chased each other round the house till their grandparents asked them to be quiet for a while.

Banoo and Rustom spoilt their grandchildren. They bought them new toys and new clothes. They took them out to the shops, unlike Mary, who had shut them in the cupboard under the stairs. The seasons ticked by, visitors came and went, neighbours popped in to see how the girls were getting on, but a time bomb was ticking under the surface. The two girls were having far too much fun to realise what was going on.

Banoo had a friend called Kathy, a young woman, in her late twenties. She always came to see Banoo on the same day, because she had to work the rest of the week. Every week, Kathy would come and visit, have some lunch and spend some time playing with the Lesley and Karen. The girls enjoyed her visits and looked forward to the next week, when Kathy would return. She was a good friend of Banoo's and the two women used to sit and chatter away, while Rustom hid himself in the shed, out of the way of this female talk. One day, Kathy came to visit as usual, but this time she stayed much longer. She arrived early in the morning, staying for lunch and then on into the evening. She seemed to be making a big fuss of Karen. Lesley was a bit put out. She couldn't understand why suddenly Kathy wasn't interested in playing with her as well. After supper, the girls had their baths and got into their pyjamas. Banoo went upstairs with Kathy and started to pack Karen's clothes into a big suitcase, then all her toys into a big box. Lesley, who had followed them, was baffled as she watched as all Karen's toys were packed into a big box. What was all this about?

Banoo took the box and Kathy took the case out to Kathy's car. Kathy came back up and said, 'It's cold out there. Karen will need something warm on.' Karen was bundled into a coat over the top of her pyjamas, a hat, her shoes, then Kathy wrapped a blanket around her and carried her out to the car. Karen smiled – she loved being with Kathy. Not a word was said as the door closed.

Lesley looked at her grandmother. 'Where is Karen going, Grandma?' she asked.

Banoo put her arms around Lesley's shoulders. 'Karen has gone to live with Kathy, darling. You'll be living here with us on your own from now on.' Lesley was very confused. First her father had gone, now her sister. What on earth was going on in this family? She would find out only too soon, and then she would wish she could hide in the cupboard under the stairs and never come out.

Chapter 3

Lesley is Introduced to Her Abusers

---•⚬⚬•---

The months ticked by and although Lesley missed Karen she quite liked being spoilt by her grandparents. She soon settled down to life without her sister. She adored Banoo and Rustom – they were very kind and loving and looked after her well. Banoo would do her hair every day and she bought ribbons and clips for her, while Rustom took her out on his insurance rounds in his little car. She wondered where Karen was, but she was having too much fun for it to worry her. Lesley didn't miss the endless arguments her parents used to have, or being shut in the cupboard while her mother disappeared for hours. Life was good.

Lesley got to know the neighbours quite well. Rustom had bought her a pedal car, which she loved to play on out in the street. Lesley loved *Z-Cars*, and could quite often be seen running up the back of the neighbours' heels in her prized possession, whilst belting out the theme tune to this show and shouting, 'You're nicked!' Fortunately, the neighbours were very kind and didn't mind this boisterous little girl racing up and down.

Life was good fun and Lesley was getting older, looking forward to staying with her grandparents and going to school. Then, like a cold wind from the North, bringing the devil on horseback, the thing called Pam arrived. Lesley would remember that day for the rest of her life. The day

Pam arrived was the day that Lesley first felt real fear. Pam's arrival in the house that day was a very bad omen for this little girl. During the next eleven years of her life, Lesley would come to realise that she was right to be afraid of her. As soon as Pam arrived, the usually relaxed, warm feeling in the house seemed to be sucked out in an instant, as if some supernatural force had entered the house and cast an evil spell over its occupants. Lesley thought that Pam looked quite young, although she wore her hair scraped back in a severe bun on top of her head.

Suddenly, Banoo and Rustom were finding fault with everything Lesley did. 'Sit up straight at the table,' Banoo barked. Lesley could not remember ever hearing her grandmother shout at her, she was shocked. Who was this evil creature?

Then it was Rustom's turn. 'Hold your knife properly!' he shouted. Lesley was horrified. This was totally alien to the gentle grandparents Lesley had known, and she was not at all comfortable with the new situation. This stranger had arrived in the house and cast an ice spell over her normally loving, kind grandparents. Lesley decided she really did not like this woman.

And then it happened, and in that one moment, time stood still and horror and fear became a reality. Pam said to Banoo, 'Shall I put Lesley to bed tonight? It will give you a much-needed break.' Lesley started to feel uneasy.

'Oh, yes please, if you don't mind. Lesley is a good girl, she can get herself ready for bed.'

Lesley was horrified! She didn't even know who this woman was, where she had come from, or what she was doing here. She ran to her grandmother for comfort.

'Grandma, please take me to bed, please, please,' she pleaded.

Banoo patted her hand and said, 'Run along, darling. You only have to get your pyjamas on and clean your teeth. Pam will look after you.'

How Lesley would grow to despise that name in years to come. She would also fear bedtime every day until she was a teenager. For tonight, she would have to tolerate this thing called Pam. Lesley started to climb the stairs, slowly, as if she hoped that Pam would change her mind and go back downstairs, sending a weary Banoo to take her place.

All of a sudden, Lesley felt an iron hand around the back of her neck. 'Come on, you little bitch. Move, quickly'. Lesley let out a scream, she felt sure this monster called Pam had come here to kill her. 'Shut up, or I'll give you something to yell about!' Pam said.

Lesley was upset. She had never been mistreated or had violence used against her by her parents or her grandparents. 'Go away, I hate you, I hate you!' Lesley cried. From out of nowhere, a hand flew towards her face. Lesley didn't see it coming, but she felt it. She was suddenly aware of a stinging pain like she had never known before. Lesley sobbed as she changed into her nightclothes. She crossed the landing to clean her teeth, only too aware that Pam was watching her every move. 'Come along, girl. I haven't got all night!' she barked. Lesley cleaned her teeth and ran back to her bedroom, very quickly, in case she got another slap.

That night this little four-year-old realised that the thing called Pam was an evil, cruel bitch. She cried herself to sleep, burying her sore little face in the pillow. The next morning, Lesley gingerly came down the stairs to breakfast. She looked left and right before going into the kitchen, to check whether Pam was lurking anywhere nearby, waiting to slap her again.

To her relief, Lesley found her grandmother making a pot of tea and some toast. 'Good morning, my darling,' Banoo said, giving Lesley a big cuddle and holding her tight. Lesley thought that if she told her grandma what Pam had done she would send the horrible woman away.

'I'm sure she didn't mean to hurt you' Banoo said when Lesley had finished.

'But Grandma,' Lesley said indignantly, 'she put her arms round my neck like this!' She put her tiny hands round Banoo's neck to demonstrate.

'Oh, I'm sure it wasn't that bad,' her grandmother said. Lesley was really confused now. She had been smacked in the face, grabbed round the neck and her grandmother thought that this was acceptable behaviour! She took herself off into the living room to sit and eat her breakfast alone and try and figure out what was happening to her cosy little life.

A few days later, with Lesley having escaped further abuse, the thing called Pam headed home to Scotland. Lesley thought Scotland must be where the devil lives! She had no idea where it was, but she hoped it was so far away that this evil woman would never come and visit again. Lesley breathed a sigh of relief as Pam climbed into a taxi and Banoo closed the front door. The house settled back into its normal peaceful routine and Rustom and Banoo went back to their usual chirpy selves. But it wasn't long before another visitor arrived. This time, the visitor was a man.

Rustom and Banoo had mentioned someone called Nuri while they were talking to Pam. He seemed to be in his thirties and very smartly dressed but not much hair, which Lesley found quite amusing. He wasn't at all like the horrid woman who had just visited. He made Lesley laugh, he sat her on his lap, and he played games with her. Lesley liked him, she decided. How wrong her misplaced trust would prove to be within the next two months.

The man stayed for a week. As he was leaving, suitcase in hand, Grandma called out, 'Give our love to Pam!' and Granddad called, 'See you soon!' Lesley's heart skipped a beat. Surely this kind, funny man couldn't seriously be married to the thing called Pam? He was just too nice. Lesley wondered what had her grandfather meant by 'See you soon'. How soon? See them where? Lesley's little brain went into meltdown. She was a very worried little girl – and she was right to be worried. A few weeks later, Lesley's life would be changed forever and it would take her years to forgive her grandparents for making their decision – a decision which would cause Lesley many years of abuse and misery.

*

Lesley didn't like the noises or the smells around her. Banoo had to keep a tight hold of her hand. The coach station was crammed with smelly old crates that hissed when the brakes were applied and spat diesel out of their exhaust pipes. The coaches were all different colours, with funny writing on their sides. Lesley couldn't read properly yet, so she didn't know what the words were, which was a blessing really. The sudden hiss of the brakes made Lesley jump; she was not at all happy being in this place. Her grandmother had packed her a suitcase, dressed her in her very best clothes and bought her some new shoes to wear. Lesley thought that if one of these noisy coaches were to get too close it would put black diesel spots on her lovely new pink cardigan. She tried to hide behind her grandmother's coat so that she was protected from the hisses and spits of diesel around her.

Lesley thought she was going on holiday; she couldn't think why else she would be going on a coach trip with her grandma.

'Grandma, Grandma, where are we going?' she asked Banoo.

'I'll tell you when we get on the coach, darling,' her grandmother replied. 'It's a surprise.'

Lesley thought it must be a very special holiday. Banoo, on the other hand, knew that if she told her granddaughter where she was taking her, Lesley might start screaming the place down, or, worse still, she might run off and something terrible happen to her.

'But Grandma, why can't Granddad drive us to where we're going?'

Banoo tried not to let Lesley hear the tremble in her voice. She cursed her husband for making her do this journey alone with their granddaughter. She could have done with his moral support, or someone to answer a few of Lesley's many questions. She stopped and turned to Lesley, 'It's too far, my darling. Besides, Granddad has to go to work.'

'So where are we going, Grandma? Please tell me.' Lesley was asking again.

Her grandmother composed herself once more and said calmly, 'Not yet, darling. Now stay close to me, or you might be run over by a coach and that will never do.' Lesley would recall this conversation – and in particular that sentence – many times throughout her life and would wish she had been run over by a coach.

Eventually, after struggling their way through the crowds of travellers, Banoo found the right coach. It was a black one with a funny little dog on the side. The driver took their tickets and told Banoo to leave the suitcase by the coach and that he would put it in the luggage compartment under the coach in a minute. Lesley was excited, but she couldn't understand why Grandma didn't have a suitcase too. She forgot to ask, too busy thinking about the trip ahead.

The driver smiled down at her. 'Going on your holidays, little lady?' he asked.

Lesley beamed up at him. 'Yes, I'm going with my grandma,' she said proudly.

The driver smiled. 'Off you go, then. Your seat numbers are on the tickets,' he said. Banoo walked down the coach, looking at all the seat numbers. Eventually they found their seats, a few rows from the front, on the same side as the driver.

'Here we are, dear. These are our seats,' Banoo said. She pointed to the seat by the window. 'You sit there. You can watch the world go by till it gets dark.'

Lesley was not very impressed with the coach. It smelt funny and the lady in front of them had some really strong perfume on that made her feel queasy. Lesley knelt up on her seat and looked around her. There were coaches of every colour and people everywhere around the coach station. She looked into the coach opposite theirs, where a little boy was sticking his tongue out at her. Lesley smiled coyly and did likewise, without her grandmother noticing. The boy's mother realised what was going on and gave him a slap, which made Lesley smile. She looked down the coach. She could see the tops of heads and hear lots of chatter in a funny accent. She couldn't work out where these people were from.

As they eased their way out of Victoria coach station in the evening sunshine, Lesley still had that unanswered question in her head. Where were they going? The coach pulled out onto the streets of London. People were going about their business, though some stopped to watch the coach pass by, no doubt wishing they were on it too. 'So Grandma, where are we going? Will there be a beach there?' Banoo looked very serious now. Lesley sensed that all was not well. This was not an expression Lesley had seen before.

Banoo started to speak, and as she did, Lesley realised where she was going: a place called hell. 'Now, listen carefully, my darling. Granddad and I are not getting any younger. In fact, we are both too old to be looking after a little girl like you. We have decided that you would be better off with another family.' Lesley opened her mouth to speak, but her grandmother was determined to get this over with as quickly and painlessly as possible. 'Let me finish darling. Your mummy can't look after you because Daddy is not around to help her. She has no money and she couldn't afford to keep you or Karen, that's why Karen went to live with Kathy. Granddad has to go to work, so I would have to take you and pick you up from school. I'm far too old for that. I brought your mummy up, but I was much younger then. Granddad and I have found you a good home. They are good people who will adopt you and bring you up as their own, just as Kathy has done with Karen.'

Lesley was worried now. Who were these 'good' people and where were they?

'You are going to live in Scotland with Pam and Nuri. They will send you to school and bring you up to be a good person.'

Lesley could not believe what her grandmother had just told her. Her grandparents were throwing her into the jaws of hell, to live with Pam and her husband. Lesley started to cry as the realisation of what was happening hit her. She sobbed so loudly that several people on the coach asked Banoo what was wrong, to which Banoo made excuses.

The little girl was inconsolable. 'No! No! No! You can't send me there! She hates me! She'll kill me!'

Banoo wished she could turn the clock back and put everything back as it was, but that was impossible now that Raymond was dead. She hugged her granddaughter and told her she would be fine. Lesley did not believe a word she said. The two people she worshipped and adored were sending her to live with a monster! Lesley was terrified, and rightly so. At that moment, all the love she had ever felt for her grandparents died. Not forever, but at this point in her life, she had been let down by the only two people in her life she had ever trusted. They must be insane to think that she could ever be happy living in the same house as the thing called Pam. That would never happen. Never, never ever. She stared out into the darkness, crying as the coach sped through the countryside and eventually cried herself to sleep as they passed Gretna Green.

The overnight coach journey seemed to last forever, broken up only when the driver stopped somewhere during the night for everyone to stretch their legs and use the facilities.

Daylight dawned and the sun came up slowly over the horizon, like a great golden ball in the sky. The birds were chirping and the flowers at the roadside turned their little heads towards the sun to make the most of this new day. There wasn't a cloud in the sky; it was going to be a glorious day. Some people on the coach were chatting excitedly about all the places they wanted to visit in Scotland, looking forward to having a lovely holiday. Some were going to visit family members in Scotland, they were very excited and could not wait to reach their destination.

Lesley did not share this happy mood. Every mile the coach travelled north brought more fear and trepidation. She tried to convince herself that this was a bad dream and that she might wake up in a minute, but she knew the reality was very different.

They had to disembark at Glasgow and then jump on a train to Motherwell, where Pam lived with Nuri. Lesley listened to the clackety-clack of the train wheels on the track, each mile bringing her ever closer to hell. The train arrived into Motherwell station and Banoo trudged up the steep steps from the platform to road level, where she hailed a taxi to take them to Jerviston Street. The taxi left the station and turned left into Merry Street. There were shops on both sides of the road and Lesley's eyes were drawn to Onesti's Fish Bar, a place she would get to know well in the next few years. The taxi continued down Merry Street, which seemed to go on forever. Lesley wondered how much further they were going.

The driver crossed Calder Bridge and pointed to the big green area on the right. 'That's Calder Park. You'll love it there. There are swings and a roundabout – my children love going there,' he said.

Lesley couldn't imagine how she would ever love anything in this strange town. The car turned left after Calder Bridge and up a small incline into Jerviston Street. The house was nearly at the end on the left-hand side. Banoo paid the taxi driver and took hold of the suitcase. Lesley climbed out of the taxi. She did not like what she saw. The house had a very high wall, and to this little girl it looked like a prison wall, grey and intimidating. They went through the big wooden gates into a long driveway, Lesley wondered if the drive led straight into the jaws of hell.

The house was the biggest building Lesley had ever seen, except Buckingham Palace! It looked cold, uninviting and unfriendly. Probably like the people who live here, Lesley thought to herself. As they walked up the long driveway to the door, Lesley noticed a huge garage to the left of the drive, although there was no car in it. There was a greenhouse, which seemed a very strange thing to have in a front garden. Some of the panes of glass were missing and the door was hanging off it. There seemed to be doors all along the front and side of the house and a path on either side. It felt sinister and Lesley was very frightened. Banoo walked to the front door, Lesley trailing behind, the reluctant victim in this plot. The door opened and there it stood: the thing called Pam. Lesley decided she hated this place before they had even crossed the threshold!

The house in Jerviston Street, where I was abused. Left downstairs window was the lounge; right downstairs window was the piano room; left upstairs window was Pam and Nuri's room; right upstairs window was the spare room.

'Welcome!' Pam said. She spoke in a posh accent, not like Lesley or her family and certainly not like that funny accent Lesley had been listening to on the coach. Lesley wondered whether she would have to learn a whole new language to survive in this foreign place called Scotland. 'I'll make a pot of tea, and I baked some cakes especially for you. You must be hungry after that long trip.'

Lesley tried to imagine what might be in the cakes. Snails? Frogs? Spiders? She clung to her grandmother's skirt.

'Come on, dear,' Banoo said. 'Look what Pam has baked, just for you.'

Lesley wasn't about to be won over by a bit of cake, so she pulled a face and said, 'Don't want any.'

The two women sat and chatted about how Lesley had been so upset about coming to live here and how Banoo had made sure she had enough clothes till Pam and Nuri could buy her some more.

'Don't be so silly,' Pam said, with an evil smirk on her face, 'You'll be fine here. We'll look after you.' Banoo explained how she had tried to convince Lesley that she would be fine but how Lesley seemed to think she would hate it there. Pam seemed to find that funny. Lesley couldn't understand how it could possibly be funny to be so afraid. In all the goings-on and tears about having to go there, Lesley had forgotten to ask her grandmother how long she was staying to help her settle in. She was taken aback when she realised that although her grandmother had brought her here, she was not staying the night, but returning to Reading on the overnight coach. Banoo hugged Lesley, told her to be good for her new mummy and daddy, put her coat on and then she was gone.

Lesley started to sob very loudly. For the first time in

her short life, she was completely alone, in a strange house, in a strange town, in a strange country. She was now absolutely terror-stricken. That would not change for many years to come. 'Welcome!' Lesley heard a voice behind her. She recognised the man as Nuri. He held out his hand and Lesley gingerly took it, wondering what was coming next. 'Would you like to see your new bedroom?' he asked her.

Lesley hadn't even thought about her room. Would it be big? Would there be pretty pictures on the walls? Would she have a nice view? Although neither Lesley's parents nor her grandparents had much money, she always had pretty bedding in her room and pretty pictures on the walls.

Lesley nervously followed Nuri through the big rolling house that seemed as big as a palace! First, they went out of the kitchen door, back into the tiny hallway Lesley had first seen when they entered the house. The door she had entered through was painted dark blue, making the hallway dark. There was a funny little room to the left. It didn't have a proper door but a curtain made of brightly coloured strips of plastic. Nuri explained that this was where she should keep her coat and shoes, as he and Pam did. There was also a nondescript cupboard, filled with jars of jam and boxes of crisps. Lesley thought this must be a very funny household, if they only ate crisps and jam!

Nuri led her up two steps, into a big room with another door at the opposite end. This was the dining room. There was a huge table in the middle with eight chairs round it. Lesley found this most odd. There were only two of them, so why so many chairs? There were two windows. One overlooked the long driveway, the other seemed to over-look the passageway that ran up the side of the house. Nuri led her through the other door into a huge hallway. There were four more doors! Lesley wasn't too happy with this great sprawling house. She wanted to be back in Reading in the security of her grandma's warm, loving house. By the time that actually happened, Lesley had almost forgotten what being loved felt like. Nuri pointed to each door in turn. Lounge, piano room – so called because there was a grand piano in there that belonged to Pam's mother, Lillian – another room under the stairs, which belonged to a boy, Simon, also adopted. A bookcase under the stairs finished the tour. Except for a big glass door with an even bigger wooden outer door that led into the garden. Lesley would get to know every inch of that garden in great detail over the coming years. Lesley was amazed at the size of this place. Her grandparents' house would fit into this one three times over!

'Come on, this way.' Nuri was off again. They climbed the first staircase, it came to a stop and Lesley found herself on a landing, looking up at another landing with another three doors and a great big cupboard. Nuri was pointing now. 'On the left, there, that is the toilet. Next to it is the bathroom. The other room is what we call the junk room. Pam stores some of her clothes in that cupboard.' Lesley was sure she would get lost in this great big unfriendly, cold house. Nuri turned on his heel and climbed the last staircase. 'Don't worry,' he said. 'You'll soon get to know your way around.' Lesley followed him up the staircase to another big landing and found herself looking at another five doors. She thought maybe she was dreaming this and it was really the devil's house, full of trickery. She expected a great big tree to suddenly appear and lots of horned creatures to start running in and out of the rooms! Nuri opened the first door on the left. 'This is your room. What do you think?' he asked Lesley. She walked past him into the room. It was square and one part of the ceiling sloped downwards which seemed odd to this little girl. There was a small window, from which she could see the gardens all along the street. She turned round and looked at the room. They had made her bed and it had a plain pink candlewick bedspread on it. There was a wooden chest of drawers, a little wooden wardrobe with a drawer underneath it and a wooden chair. None of the furniture had any colour. The walls were all woodchip wallpaper, white and very austere. There were no toys, no books, no teddy bears, nothing that made it look remotely homely or welcoming for a small child.

'Well, what do you think?' Nuri asked. Lesley was careful with her reply; she didn't want another slap on her first night there! 'It's … it's … um … nice,' she eventually replied. Lesley thought in her little head that maybe this was all a mistake and Grandma and Granddad would miss her so much, they would come and take her back to Reading. If only that had been the case.

Nuri showed her the other rooms. They were all huge, but there was nobody sleeping in any of them except for the one in the opposite corner to Lesley's, which was Pam and Nuri's room. There was another cupboard, crammed full of books. Lesley thought this was a very strange house indeed. It was nothing like the home she was used to, full of warmth, love and laughter.

Lesley did not sleep that first night. Her head was full of questions. Why had her daddy died? Why didn't her mummy want her? Where was her sister? Was she in another great big house somewhere far away? What was she doing here? How long would she have to stay here before she could go back to her grandparents?

Chapter 4

The Beatings and Cruelty Start

———— ⟨⚬⟩ ————

Lesley felt very tired as she made her way to the kitchen in the morning. She feared she would get lost in this house one day – it was massive! Breakfast was very difficult for Lesley. She hadn't slept and she felt homesick for Banoo's lovely house in Reading. She missed being cuddled and she was missing her toys. Pam made her a cup of tea and a slice of toast. Lesley ate nervously, terrified that if she did or said the wrong thing she would get another slap.

When breakfast was finished, Nuri took her into the big garden. Suddenly, from out of nowhere, two great big dogs came running at her. Lesley screamed and ran back into the house, with the dogs in hot pursuit. Nuri came to fetch Lesley, who was shaking uncontrollably with fright, to take her out into the garden. 'Meet Suki and Pancho,' he said. 'Come here, Suki. Come and meet your new friend. Come on, Pancho. You have a new playmate.' Lesley gingerly reached out to touch Suki. She was huge, a Great Dane, towering over Lesley. Then Pancho came to say hello. He was a boxer dog, much more gentle and easy-going in temperament. Lesley soon forgot her fears and sat down to stroke the two dogs while Nuri chattered about how happy she would be in her new home. What a great big lie that would prove to be.

The next night, Pam suggested that Lesley might like to have a bath. Lesley was not comfortable with this idea, given the episode in Reading, when she experienced violence at bedtime. She slowly followed Pam to the bathroom. Pam ran the bath and Lesley undressed and lowered herself nervously into the water. 'Now, then,' Pam said. 'Let's see how clean you are, shall we?' She took the loofah from the ledge and started to scrub Lesley's neck. Lesley tried hard not to cry, but it hurt because the loofah was hard and it felt more like being scraped with sandpaper. Pam stopped and with a satisfied voice said, 'Now you're clean!'

Next came the hair wash. Lesley's grandma and mum had always tilted her head backwards so that the shampoo would not sting her eyes. That was not going to happen here. Pam grabbed the plastic jug that sat on the side of the bath. She filled it full to the brim and tipped it straight over the top of Lesley's head. Never having been treated like this before, Lesley was frightened and shocked at the same time. She spluttered and tried to rub the water out of her eyes and brush her hair back off her face, swallowing mouthfuls of water at the same time. She started to cry, and the gasping and sobbing made her swallow more water. Pam was oblivious to the little girl's discomfort and carried on, applying shampoo which stung Lesley's eyes and made her cry more. Lesley tried to wipe the shampoo out of her eyes, but her hands were covered in bubbles so it made the stinging worse. She begged Pam to stop for a moment so that she could clear her eyes. She asked for a flannel to hold over her eyes, but instead of replying or agreeing to her request, Pam grabbed a hairbrush from the shelf over the sink and belted Lesley round the back of the head with it. 'For goodness' sake child, stay still!' she bellowed. Lesley hadn't seen this coming and she wept as she remembered a similar pain when this monster had slapped her in her own home. The ordeal ended when another full jug of water was emptied over her head and a dry flannel thrown at her. Lesley was crying, tears of despair. She had thought that this woman was the monster from hell and it had just been proved to her.

Suddenly she was aware of Pam barking, 'I hope we're not going to have this performance every time you have your hair washed.' Lesley smiled lamely. She hated this woman, she was evil, nasty and cruel. She dried herself off and changed into her nightclothes. 'Come downstairs when you're dressed. I'll make you a cup of hot chocolate.' Lesley went downstairs and sat drinking her hot chocolate, her little heart pounding with fear lest she upset Pam and incur more pain. Her heart was breaking and she longed for a cuddle from her grandparents. Little did she know, it was going to be a very long wait before anyone ever cuddled her again.

The hair-washing ordeal was repeated every bath time. Lesley grew to dread bath nights. She tried her hardest not to mind the jug full of water being tipped over her head, but it didn't get any easier. She longed for her grandma to come and rescue her from this place.

She was always being told off. Pam and Nuri told her off for everything. They tried to get her to talk posh, like they did. Words were corrected time and time again, till Lesley thought she was going slowly mad! They told her off if she made too much noise chewing her food. They told her off for not holding her cutlery properly, but it was how she had been shown at home and nobody had ever told her off before. Worst of all, some of the food she was expected to eat was not fit to feed a dog! Lesley had never been a great eater, she had always been a bit choosy over what she liked and didn't like, but her mother and grandmother had never made a fuss and just let her eat as much or little as she wanted. Pam was different. If Lesley did not eat every last morsel on the plate, Pam would pull her head back by her hair, and ram the food into her mouth. Lesley would then start to gag and quite often she was sick, which then made Pam so angry she would drag Lesley off the chair and start kicking her on the floor.

Eventually, things were so bad that Lesley was hardly eating at all, mainly because she was so terrified of Pam's temper. Pam and Nuri decided Lesley should see a doctor. Lesley just thought she should be left alone to eat as much or as little as she wanted. Sometimes, when Pam and Nuri weren't looking, Lesley would give her unwanted food to Suki and Pancho, who were always willing to demolish any scraps they could find. Sometimes the food was so bad that even the dogs wouldn't eat it! The doctor sent Lesley for an X-ray, then for a barium meal X-ray, where she had to drink some disgusting liquid, then be turned upside down on a machine so that they could see where the blockage was, if there was one at all. Pam was livid. 'If they find out there's nothing wrong with you, God help you,' she said to Lesley. Lesley prayed that there was something wrong and she would be spared. Unfortunately, the x-rays revealed no problems and the force-feeding continued for months afterwards. Every mealtime was a battle, Pam force-feeding Lesley and Lesley throwing up all over the floor. In the end, Nuri said that Lesley was to sit in the kitchen until she finished her food. Lesley devised a plan whereby she could hide food in her pockets or throw it out of the kitchen window for the birds to eat, or give it to the dogs. She even flushed food down the toilet when she could get away with it. Lesley was determined that she wasn't going to give in to these monsters.

Lesley aged four, now adopted.

Lesley realised very quickly that violence was going to become a part of her everyday routine, in the same way that she washed her face or brushed her teeth every day. The slightest step out of line, or failure to show respect, would be met with a slap or a punch in the back. The newly adopted Lesley was about to celebrate her fifth birthday, but this birthday and every one thereafter would only bring more beatings. Lesley's fifth birthday, in August 1963, dawned and she waited for her birthday cards and presents from her mum and grandparents. Pam and Nuri didn't say a word, no mention of 'Happy Birthday', or it being a special day. Lesley was puzzled. She had always been the centre of attention on her birthday, but this was very different.

Lesley took some time to wander round the big garden, which she would grow to hate in future years. She realised that the garden was on two levels. There was one garden at the back, laid to two lawns, with a path down the middle. There were flower borders around both lawns, with two more borders on the outer boundaries to the neighbours' fences. Some stairs led down to the lower level, which led to a brook at the end of it. It was all overgrown with nettles and marsh grasses. It certainly didn't look very inviting. Lesley imagined the devil riding up on a canoe every night to give Pam instructions on how to inflict more unpleasantness on her.

She walked wearily back up to the big house and wondered whether anyone had remembered her birthday. After lunch, she was summoned to the lounge. There, in the middle of the floor, was a pretty orange dress, with lovely embroidery on it, some patent shoes with a big buckle, a blackboard on an easel with a packet of chalks and some new pyjamas. Lesley was instructed to change into the dress and try the shoes on, which she did without protest, as any protest would either have been met with a slap or ignored completely. Pam explained that she loved making clothes and had made the dress especially for Lesley, including the pretty embroidery on the front. Lesley asked who all the other presents were from.

Pam was gloating. 'They're from Nuri and myself, dear,' she said.

Lesley couldn't help herself. 'Where are my presents from my mummy and my grandma and granddad?' she asked.

Pam hissed at her. 'From now on you will not mention any of your family in my house, is that clear?'

Lesley was not happy with this reply and voiced her discontent. 'You're not my mummy. My mummy is kind and gentle, and she never hit me!'

Pam's mood changed in an instant and she turned red with rage and grabbed the little girl's arm, digging her painted bright red talon-shaped nails into Lesley's delicate skin. Lesley yelped and started to cry as the sharp nails broke her skin and blood appeared on her arm. 'You ungrateful little bitch! We rescued you from poverty and gave you a home! If it wasn't for us you'd be on the streets!' she screamed. 'If you want any birthday cake, you had better start acting like you're grateful.'

Lesley knew she was beaten. She never found out whether her family had sent any cards or presents and she didn't dare ever ask again. She went to bed that night and cried. Lesley couldn't understand why her grandparents would want to abandon her to this horrid place and these vile people. She dreaded what the rest of her life would be like in this house. Little did she know just how bad it would get; this was just the start of eleven years of hell for this child.

The rest of the month passed by, and Lesley had to start school in Motherwell. She liked the look of the school, Calder Primary School in Draffen Street. It was a small school and Lesley liked that it was not too far to walk from the house in Jerviston Street. Lesley only had to walk over Calder Bridge, then cross Merry Street at the end and turn left. The building was compact, with classrooms in a square, all opening out onto the assembly hall on the ground floor. A mezzanine landing on the upper level gave the classrooms upstairs a bird's-eye view of the hall below.

The teachers seemed nice. Mr. Baird, the headmaster, was a very nice man. He knew all the children's names and always had time to stop and chat to them as he passed by. Lesley's classmates were not at all happy that they had an English girl in their class and they let her know this in no uncertain terms. They called her Little Black Sambo and Nigger, which was not only deplorable but ridiculous, as she was not black but of Asian descent, her dark skin having been passed down from the Iranian side of the family. Lesley found the racist jibes extremely hurtful. This was the 1960s when racism was still very prevalent in communities around the country, especially in the smaller communities in Scotland. Eventually, Lesley made friends and the racist children found other children to pick on.

At home, Lesley was gradually introduced to the rest of the family. There were Pam's parents, Lillian and Harry. She liked them; they were nothing like Pam, and Lesley wondered how such a lovely couple could possibly have produced such a monster of a daughter. They lived in Harrogate in Yorkshire, where they owned a tiny grocery store, and Lesley was taken on holiday to visit them. They allowed her to sell the penny sweets, and eat some as well! When Pam wasn't looking, Lillian would give Lesley a bag of sweets and tell her to hide them, in case she got told off by Pam. Harry was a chain-smoker. He reeked of cigarettes; the acrid smell seemed to be in everything. It was in the shop, in the house, even the bedding smelt of cigarettes. Lesley decided cigarettes were horrible things and vowed she would never smoke – a vow she kept throughout her life.

Nuri's parents lived in Dumfries, near to Nuri's sister Golly and her husband Alan. Golly wasn't her proper name, but she had an Iranian name nobody could say or spell, so she was always called Golly. Her parents had a beautiful rose garden which was lovingly tended by Nuri's father. Golly and Nuri's parents seemed to be very old, always ill and very grumpy.

Lesley settled into life in the big house very uneasily. She never felt comfortable and felt that she always had to be on her best behaviour. She wasn't allowed to run in the house, or sing or play, like her schoolfriends. Instead she had to sit and read, learning new words and the meaning of those words, then she had to write her letters, over and over until Pam decided her writing was neat enough. The rules for being an acceptable child in the Baha'i faith were drummed into her. She must only speak when spoken to; she must not accept food until everyone else had theirs; she must remember to say please and thank you; she must give up her seat to an adult if there were not enough chairs.

Lesley thought this place felt like a prison camp compared to Banoo's easy-going, warm, loving home. She was only five, but her childhood was going to be taken away from her, all too quickly. She was always being made to learn, long after her homework was completed. Pam would check her homework, and if it was not up to her standard she would tear the page out, give Lesley a hefty slap and make her do it all again. Lesley soon realised that Pam was a living monster. Worse still, she discovered that Pam was a schoolteacher, who taught domestic science at a local high school. Given some of the food that was placed on the table at mealtimes, Lesley wondered how she had ever managed to teach others how to cook! Lesley prayed that she would never be a pupil in one of Pam's classes. She could just imagine the ridicule when she was shouted at in front of everyone!

Lesley liked her teacher at Calder Primary. Mrs. Crosby was a gentle, soft-spoken lady and all the children loved her. One day, Mrs. Crosby handed out some exercise books. 'Now then, children,' she said, 'I want you to cover these school books at home, with your mummies and daddies. They will show you how to do it.' Lesley went home, dreading the fact that she would have to ask not only for some spare brown paper or wallpaper to cover her books, but for help to do this. She nervously asked at teatime whether she could use any unwanted wallpaper. 'Of course,' Nuri said. Then she asked for help to complete the task.

'I'm afraid Pam will have to help you,' he said. 'I'm useless at covering books.'

When the dinner plates were washed and put away, Pam brought a spare roll of wallpaper in and put it on the table. 'I will show you what to do, then you can go ahead and have a go,' she said.

Lesley was nervous, she knew she had to pay close attention or she would be in big trouble! She watched as Pam folded this way, then that, then made a tiny cut. She folded all the edges in and neatly stuck a piece of Sellotape on the cover to hold it in place. Lesley tried to copy her. She measured out the paper as Pam had done, very carefully, then cut the edge so that it would fold into the corner. She folded the main piece over and ran her finger along it, just as she had been shown. She showed Pam, for whom perfection was the only option. Lesley watched in horror as the carefully folded cover was torn off the book and it was thrown back at her. 'Rubbish!' barked Pam. 'Do it again!'

And so it was that this little five-year-old, with tears in her eyes, sat till ten o'clock that night, doing the same cover over and over until Pam decided it was good enough. Lesley grew to hate the new school terms, when books would be issued by the teachers with instructions to cover them. She knew that every year would be the same – hours of covering and recovering till Pam decided her covers passed.

Lesley presented her book to Mrs. Crosby the next morning, yawning as she did so. If only her teacher knew what torture she had endured to get to this point.

The school year was relatively uneventful. Books were sent home with Lesley for her to read and learn the words, which, on the whole, she managed successfully. Lesley was a bright girl and would ask for library books to read too. The end of year came and the children all went home for the long summer holidays. Lesley was excited; all those weeks of not having any schoolwork meant she had lots of time to play and meet up with her school friends. That was what she thought, but Pam had other ideas.

The first day of the holidays, Pam called Lesley into the kitchen. 'Now, then,' she said. 'As you have nothing to do all summer, I am not having you idling around the place causing trouble. This is an ideal time for you to learn how to do the weeding. Come into the garden and I will show you what needs doing'.

Lesley's heart sank. She'd seen her granddad cut the lawn and tend to his prized roses, but she had no idea what a weed might be. She followed Pam outside into the front garden. Lesley had discovered that although the front door was actually at the rear of the house, the piece of garden where the driveway garage were situated was known as the front garden. The garden where the front door was, on the other hand, was known as the back garden. It seemed very strange to Lesley that the house had been built back to front. The front garden was huge and Lesley thought that if she had to spend the summer holidays weeding she would be worn out! She watched as Pam pulled a couple of weeds out and pointed to areas of the garden where the weeds had grown tall and spread. 'Do this rockery today. You can do the fruit patch tomorrow,' she said.

Lesley started to pull up the weeds. She could hear the children out in the street, laughing and shrieking as they chased each other up and down. Across the road from the big house was a golf course. The children in the street had pulled the wire fence from its moorings over the years, so now they could climb underneath and run onto the golf course behind the bushes and trees. The children loved to steal any golf balls they saw lying around, dissecting them and pulling out the rubber bands inside. The golfers would get very angry if they caught them. At the end of the road was a glen, with trees and a stream and waterfall.

Lesley wished she could run out into the street to play as well, but she didn't dare. Instead, she pulled some weeds up and put them in the bucket; she didn't want Pam to think she hadn't been working. Every now and again, one of her friends would shout through the big wooden gates, but Lesley didn't dare answer, too afraid of Pam to risk being accused of laziness. Suki and Pancho wandered up to have a sniff around and they lay down close to her, watching as she pulled out the weeds. Lesley had got used to the dogs; they were better company than the humans in the house.

It started to rain but Lesley didn't dare go indoors. Just being in the same room as Pam frightened her. Instead she took cover amongst the tall flowers. She sat down on a rock and waited for the rain to pass. Her mind wandered back to happier times and that question that would haunt her for many years. How did her daddy die? She'd never known anyone die of a tummy ache. Maybe when she was older she would find out. Maybe the monster called Pam had killed him so that she could take over Lesley's life and keep her as a servant.

41

Lesley sighed. She missed her mum a little bit, but she missed her grandparents terribly. She wondered if she would ever see them again. Lesley's thoughts turned to her sister. Where was she? Was she having a better life than Lesley? She sincerely hoped so. Surely one of them must have gone to a loving home.

Just as Lesley was contemplating what life would be like if her dad was still alive, she was fiercely pulled from her perch, not by the arm, but by the hair. She screamed out, at which point a hand slapped her face. Lesley looked round in stunned horror. It was Pam. 'I thought I told you to do the weeding, girl' she yelled. 'Instead of that, you're sitting here doing nothing!' Her face was purple with rage and Lesley almost laughed out loud, but didn't dare.

'I was weeding, honestly, but it started to rain and my back hurt. I had only just sat down,' Lesley said lamely. She knew that no matter what she said, it wasn't going to save her.

'Shut up, you lazy little bitch!' Pam shouted. 'You wait till Nuri gets home. You're going to get such a beating.'

Lesley was really frightened, she had no idea what a beating was; neither her parents nor her grandparents had ever smacked her, never mind beaten her. She didn't like the sound of this at all. Over the next eleven years, Lesley would understand only too well what beatings were, as they became a daily occurrence.

Pam sent Lesley back into the garden in the rain, but this time Lesley worked hard, even though she was soaked to the skin. She made sure she didn't stop at all; she felt tired but fear kept her outside till the bed was finished and all the weeds were gone. She was made to forfeit lunch as a punishment, but she didn't mind that, as long as she didn't have to have the beating.

Nuri arrived home from work every evening at 5.30 pm. His routine was always the same. He would take his flask and sandwich box into the kitchen and put them by the sink, ready for being washed. Then he took his shoes off and put them in the cloakroom. He went upstairs, had a quick wash and changed into his casual clothes for the evening. They all sat down at the dinner table.

'Lesley, what did you do today?' Nuri asked her. Lesley shifted uncomfortably in her seat. Did he know that she had to receive a beating tonight? Had Pam telephoned him at work and told him to be ready for this big event, the first beating of this child they had ripped away from a loving home?

Lesley took a deep breath and answered, 'I've been weeding today.'

'That's very good. How much did you do?' Nuri asked.

Lesley looked at Pam, her face looking like she might explode. 'Not ... Not very much,' Lesley replied. 'I have never done weeding before. It was hard and I stopped because it was raining and I was tired.'

Pam let out a guffaw. 'Huh! I caught the lazy bitch, sitting on a rock gazing at the flowers.'

'Never mind,' Nuri replied. 'You'll just have to work harder tomorrow.' Lesley thought that was a great idea so she nodded. She was wondering whether the beating was still going to happen, or had she escaped it? There was going to be no second chance. Even if Nuri protested, he had to do as Pam said, otherwise she would shout at him too.

Pam washed the dinner plates and pans and Lesley dried them and put them away, her little hands trembling as they did every night. Lesley knew only too well that Pam was very easily displeased, so she was very careful not to drop anything. No words were exchanged, not that this was unusual. Lesley hated Pam and would only speak if she was spoken to. She figured if she did that, Pam would have no reason to shout at her or beat her.

Eventually Pam spoke. 'When you've put the dishes away, come to your bedroom,' she said.

'Why?' Lesley asked, terrified that she already knew the answer.

'We have the small matter of a beating to deal with, girl,' Pam said.

Lesley's legs turned to jelly. She still had no idea what this beating was, but the very word itself summoned up images of violence and pain. Lesley put the tea towel down and slowly wiped over the dining table, making sure she didn't miss any crumbs. She made sure the kitchen was tidy, then slowly, ever so slowly, she climbed the stairs.

Nuri and Pam were in her bedroom, waiting. Nuri was stood by the window. He had a funny-looking thing in his hand. Lesley had never seen one of those before. It was a shiny wooden stick with a loop at one end and a thick solid leather piece at the other end. It looked terrifying to this tiny little person. Nuri beckoned to Lesley. Pam closed her bedroom door. No escape.

'Pam tells me that you disobeyed her today,' he started. 'You didn't even do half of what you were asked to do. This will make sure you do not sit down tomorrow,' he said. He was flicking the end of this wooden thing into his hand. The leather piece made a loud thwack as it hit the palm of his hand. 'From now on,' he continued, 'each time that you disobey or misbehave, this will be your punishment.'

Lesley started to cry. She wasn't quite sure what was going to happen next, but she knew it was going to hurt.

'Pull your pants down and lay over the bed,' Nuri instructed. Lesley was so frightened that she thought she might wet herself in terror, and then they might kill her! She barely had time to get her tiny hands out of the way when the first blow hit her backside.

Lesley screamed in pain. 'Stop, please stop! It hurts. You're hurting me!' she cried, but the blows kept coming. After twelve lashes with the thing, it stopped. Lesley was crying hysterically now.

Nuri left the room and very coldly Pam said, 'Let that be a lesson to you. Now get to bed.' She left the room, slamming the door behind her.

Lesley removed her clothes and went over to the dressing table mirror. She could see her little backside in the mirror, covered in red welts from the implement. In years to come, Lesley would learn that this was called a riding crop. The forlorn little girl changed into her pyjamas and climbed into bed. She sobbed herself to sleep in her pillow and wished her captors dead. She wished her grandparents would come and rescue her from this awful house. She hated it here and she hated Pam and Nuri even more. That hatred has never subsided. Lesley felt totally alone in her life. She felt sad and longed to escape from this awful place. She had another eleven years to wait before she could leave, and she would reach the depths of despair and the brink of suicide before that day arrived.

The next morning, Lesley had her breakfast then headed out into the garden. She didn't want a repeat performance of yesterday. She pulled weeds, she picked the raspberries and strawberries and watered the flowers. She chased Suki and Pancho round the garden, keeping an eye out for Pam appearing from round the corner. Lesley talked to the dogs all the time. They were gentle and fun to be with and *they* would never hurt her. She told them how sad she was that she was brought to this awful place with these awful people, she told them she wished she could fly away and take them with her. Suki and Pancho looked at her as she spoke. They might even have understood her sadness.

Chapter 5

Lesley Runs Away

⸻⸙⸻

It didn't take Lesley long to realise that beatings could be administered for the pettiest of reasons. She was beaten for not hanging her clothes up properly, not cleaning her shoes after school, leaving the bedroom window open at night even though she was hot, leaving a book under the bed even though she was reading it, not putting washing in the linen basket on the correct day, not taking a bath on her allocated evening of the week. The list went on and on.

Lesley, aged seven, with her only companions Suki and Pancho.

Over the months, Lesley got to know the strange boy, Simon, who lived in the room under the stairs. He had just started at Dalziel High School. He never got any beatings, no matter what he did. Lesley didn't like him much; he was quiet and sullen and gave her the creeps. Simon never spoke about his original family and Lesley was far too afraid to ask. Over a few months of 1964 and 1965, Lesley noticed that Pam had begun to act very strangely. She seemed to be getting fat and wearing clothes that looked like a tent wrapped round her. Lesley had no understanding of what was going on, until one night when Pam disappeared. Lesley was told that she had given birth to a baby girl. Lesley was amused. This horrible violent woman now had a baby to look after. Would she beat the baby, as she had beaten Lesley?

Lesley was secretly very pleased that Pam would be in hospital for two weeks. That meant the beatings would stop for a while. Lesley was taken to be with Margaret and Eddie Sinclair, who lived further down Jerviston Street on the opposite side at number sixteen. She was instructed to stay there until Nuri returned from work in the evenings. She loved to go there after school every night as she liked being with Margaret. Margaret had the radio on and Lesley rapidly learnt the words to 'In The Middle of Nowhere' by Dusty Springfield. She could dance round the lounge with Margaret and have snacks she was never allowed at home. There were no beatings in this house and it felt warm and homely, not like her prison up the road.

The two weeks' respite passed by all too quickly and Pam returned home with her child, named Lucy. The baby screamed at all hours of the day and night, then all would go quiet. Pam moved out of the marital bedroom into the spare room opposite Lesley's. Lesley was tasked with reading to Pam while she laid in the bed cradling the baby. Lesley thought, stupidly, that a truce would now be called and she would no longer be beaten.

The summer holidays were coming to an end and it was time to go shopping for new school clothes and shoes. Lesley had grown a little over the holidays and was now approaching her seventh birthday. She was a thin little girl, so everything looked too big for her. This was not helped by the fact that Pam always bought her clothes two sizes too big, allegedly so she could grow into them! Once more her school skirt nearly reached her ankles and Lesley felt ridiculous trying it on in the shop. The shop assistant tried to convince Pam that the size below would be fine, but to no avail. The shirts were fine, as was her jumper. Pam insisted that she had lace-up shoes, which was all very well, but Lesley couldn't tie laces.

The shoes were taken home, along with the rest of her uniform. Lesley explained to Pam that she could not tie laces. 'That's fine, I will show you how,' Pam said. Unfortunately, because Lesley was so afraid of slaps and kicks, her little hands would not be still enough for her to manoeuvre her way through all the loops required to tie a lace. Every time she did it wrong, another slap would be administered. Lesley got more and more upset and totally forgot what she was supposed to be doing, so lessons were abandoned for the day with a final slap for good measure. Lesley spent the next day in the garden, weeding her allocated area for that day. After the evening meal, she was summoned to the dining room once again, to tie and untie the lace a hundred times till she finally mastered the technique. Lesley hated the shoes she had been bought. It seemed that Pam deliberately picked the most ridiculous-looking shoes she could find. She didn't dare voice her opinion; she was being beaten enough already and certainly did not want any more marks on her body.

Lesley's seventh birthday was an uneventful day, with no special treats – just the same boring practical presents. There were no dolls or nice reading books or colouring books. Lesley did not dare ask if her relatives had sent any presents, so she graciously accepted all the gifts and retreated to her bedroom. Lesley sat on her bedroom floor, thinking how nice it would have been if she could have had a teddy bear or a soft toy of some kind to cuddle. Amongst the presents was a new school satchel, which was nearly as big as Lesley. She would be forced to use this satchel until she went into her second year at secondary school. If the stitching came apart, Lesley would be made to stitch it back together, using a special leather needle with an extremely sharp point. Lesley learnt this technique very quickly, having had Pam jab her fingers with the needle if she did it wrong. Pam had no patience at all, so if Lesley didn't master something the first time round, she would be slapped and punched till she got it right.

Bearing in mind that Lesley was only just seven years old, she was summoned into the kitchen one day. Pam was doing some ironing and said to Lesley, 'Here, come and have a go at this.' Lesley was a bit scared. The iron was very hot and it hissed and spat steam and hot water. 'I will iron this handkerchief, then I will give you one to do. Watch what I do, then you can copy.' Lesley watched nervously as Pam ironed over the hankie, holding each corner as she turned it. She folded it neatly and ironed it over. 'There. Your turn,' she said to Lesley.

Lesley took the next handkerchief from the pile and opened it out. She gingerly picked up the hot iron, which immediately hissed and made her jump. She didn't like the idea of putting her fingers under the heat of the iron, so she tried to iron the hankie as it was. This was not very practical, because every time she ironed in a different direction, the hankie would move and get more creased. Pam was not amused. 'Oh for goodness' sake, child. Why are you so stupid? Watch me again, then you can do it.' Lesley watched once more, then it was her turn again. Despite her best efforts, and with Pam stood over her making her feel more afraid, Lesley had more creases in the hankie than when she started. Pam was angry now. 'Oh for God's sake!' she shouted and snatched the hankie up. Lesley wasn't quick enough. She caught her hand on the sole plate of the iron, which made her scream. 'That will teach you to be stupid!' Pam yelled and with that, she brought the iron down onto the top of Lesley's tiny hand. Lesley screamed again and started to cry. 'Get out of my sight,' Pam barked. Lesley thought she could escape to the relative safety of her bedroom so she rushed past a red-faced Pam. As she went by, Pam delivered a hefty punch to the small of her back, which sent her flying into the wall. Lesley fled the room, sobbing.

The year passed by like all of them would, with Lesley being constantly told off, constant beatings, not being allowed to have friends to play, not being allowed to go out to play. Life wasn't very nice for Lesley. She had nobody she could confide in, and even if she did, who would believe her? Lesley vowed that, one day, she would escape from this horrible house, even if it meant she had to kill Pam and Nuri to get out of there. Lucy was now two years old. Every time there was a Baha'i meeting, Lesley would be shut away in another room to play with the unruly children until the adults decided they could rejoin the main group.

Lesley returned to school after the summer holidays, wearing clothes that were too big and shoes that were too small. She always felt out of place. She was ridiculed by the other children, who couldn't understand why their mums and dads managed to buy them the right sizes in clothing, yet Lesley always looked like a coat hanger with some rags hanging on it. Pam had insisted on cutting Lesley's beautiful dark hair so short that she looked like a boy, especially with her tall, thin frame. Lesley felt ridiculous and she knew she *looked* ridiculous. All her little friends had ponytails with pretty clasps in their hair. Lesley could barely make her hair reach her ears; no wonder everyone thought she was a boy. Once, Pam sent her to Sinnet's, the newsagent just across Calder Bridge in the parade of shops. The lady served her then said, 'Okay, son, here's your change.' Lesley was mortified.

The constant beatings continued, almost on a daily basis. The slightest thing seem to send Pam into a rage, and Nuri would happily administer the necessary punishment, as if they gained some sadistic pleasure from torturing another human being. Lesley's friends didn't believe her when she told them that these people beat her, even when she showed them the bruises on her little body. That was the worst part: nobody ever believed her. The children accused her of bruising her own arms to get attention, which broke Lesley's heart. *How could these children be so cruel?* she wondered.

One of Lesley's friends, Ruth, had a birthday party coming up. Ruth gave Lesley her invitation and Lesley took it home to show Pam. She had been invited to other parties but had never been allowed to attend. This time was different. Pam liked Ruth's parents; they were well-off and quite posh and Pam liked to think that she fitted in well with the more affluent parents. 'I can't see any reason why you shouldn't go,' Pam said. 'They're good people.'

The day of the party arrived and Lesley was allowed to wear a lovely new turquoise dress Pam had made for her. It was made of lovely shiny material and had a huge pink bow round the middle. Lesley felt like the queen wearing it. Ruth's house was absolutely beautiful. It was smaller than Pam and Nuri's house, but it had a warm, welcoming feel, not like their house, which was cold and uninviting.

Lesley enjoyed the party. There were some other friends from school there and they were all allowed to play and laugh as much as they wanted. Lesley couldn't imagine Pam ever allowing that behaviour in her house! Ruth's parents didn't shout at the children, and Lesley didn't feel nervous or afraid and she loved all the party games and lovely food.

All too soon the party was over and Pam and Nuri arrived to collect Lesley. As they were going, Pam turned to Lesley and said, 'What do you say to Mrs. Clark?'

Lesley dutifully replied, 'Thank you for inviting me to Ruth's party. I had a lovely time.' Pam looked pleased that she had brought Lesley up to be polite.

The two mothers walked to the front door chatting away. As Lesley walked to the front door holding Ruth's hand, she said, 'You have a lovely house. You are very lucky.'

'Thank you. See you at school on Monday,' Ruth replied.

Lesley enjoyed the bus ride home. She couldn't remember the last time she had enjoyed herself so much. They all climbed off the bus and walked up the road. Lesley was never happy going back to that house; it felt like a prison to her. There was never any joy or love, and nobody ever showed her any affection. Lesley felt a warm glow as she remembered all the cuddles she had known as a small child, growing up with her grandparents.

Nuri reached the front door and unlocked it. As Lesley stepped inside, she suddenly felt a push and she was on the floor. Lesley hadn't seen it coming and she had tripped and hit her head on the wall in the process. She was hauled to her feet and slammed against the door. What was going on? What now? Lesley stood there, aching from the assault, her lovely dress torn, but there was worse was to come.

'So,' Pam bellowed at her, 'they have a lovely house, do they? What's wrong with this house?'

Lesley looked up at her in fear. She didn't know Pam had even heard her say those words to Ruth! She knew any reply would be the wrong one, so she said lamely, 'I'm sorry, I was just being polite. I didn't mean anything by it.' The force of the slap across her face rattled her jaw. Lesley was sure one of these days they would kill her and nobody would even know or care. Nuri lifted the riding crop from its hook in the hallway. Lesley froze. 'No, please, I didn't mean anything!' she protested, but resistance was futile. The claws that were Pam's nails dug into her arms as she was forced to climb the stairs to her bedroom for yet another beating.

On Monday, Lesley went back to school, still nursing her cuts and bruises from the brutality of the weekend. It was the day the children always had their PE lessons. Lesley got changed, amongst all the other children in the class, trying not to let anyone see the claw marks on her arms and the welts on her legs. She loved the PE lessons; the children were allowed to play around quite a bit, as long as they were careful not to hurt themselves. Lesley's arms hurt, and the big blue bruises where she had hit the floor on Saturday after the party ached. After the lesson,

Mrs. Crosby called Lesley to one side. Lesley was nervous, she didn't think she had behaved any worse than the other children in the PE lesson. Mrs. Crosby was the gentlest soul and had the patience of a saint. Lesley looked at Mrs. Crosby. She didn't look cross, so what was this about?

Mrs. Crosby beckoned Lesley to her. 'I couldn't help but notice that you have some terrible marks on your arm, dear. How did they get there?'

Lesley was afraid now. She would have to tell Mrs. Crosby about Saturday and the beating, but what would happen then? She looked down at the floor and clasped her hands tightly in front of her, feeling totally uncomfortable with the whole thing. 'Please, miss,' she said, 'I have to live with these horrid people who are not my mummy and daddy, and they beat me all the time. The bruises are where I was thrown on the floor on Saturday after Ruth's party. The scratches on my arms are where my adopted mother digs her nails into me when she gets cross.'

'Hang on, hang on,' Mrs. Crosby said. 'So where are your mum and dad?'

'My daddy died, miss, and my mummy didn't want me, so I had to come to Scotland. I hate it here! I want to go back and live with my grandma and granddad but I'm not allowed.'

Mrs. Crosby looked concerned. 'Oh dear,' she said. 'This is a sorry story. I will have to speak to these people.'

Lesley was terrified. 'Oh no, miss, you can't do that. They will beat me again and I hurt enough already.'

Mrs. Crosby was determined that she was going to speak to Pam and Nuri about the bruises, which filled Lesley with dread. She told Lesley everything would be fine and let her go. Lesley knew only too well that the outcome for her would not be a good one, but Mrs. Crosby would not be swayed. That evening, Lesley jumped every time the telephone rang. It felt as if her revelation was taunting her and she wished she had kept quiet. Then the phone rang again. Pam went out into the hall to answer it. She came back into the room and summoned Nuri into the dining room. After what felt like an eternity, Lesley was called into the room. Mrs. Crosby had told them! Oh no! Lesley vowed she would never tell anyone anything ever again. Everyone in her life she thought she could trust let her down, time after time. This time it was Mrs. Crosby who had betrayed her trust. Nuri was cross. He instructed Lesley to sit down and the lecture began.

'Lesley, why do you behave so badly and tell such awful lies about us? Mrs. Crosby says you told her we beat you and Pam dug her nails into your arms. What do you hope to achieve by telling such lies?'

Lesley looked from Nuri to Pam. She knew in that one moment, that no matter who she told about the abuse, Pam and Nuri would deny it and she would be made out to be the bad person. Lesley vowed to escape from that awful house, even if she had to kill herself. Once more, the nightly beating was dished out. Lesley hated them; she really, really hated them. She had to get to her grand-parents and safety.

Her chance came the following week. Pam and Nuri would both be late home, so she had been instructed to go to Nuri's grumpy parents, who had now moved into a big house, at number twenty-two Jerviston Street, which was further down the road on the opposite side, close to Eddie and Margaret Sinclair. Lesley wasn't going there! Lesley ate her breakfast, as she always did, but her walk to school was a brisk one. As she walked, she thought of their faces when they realised she was gone.

The school day could not pass quickly enough. When the bell rang for home time, Lesley grabbed her bag and ran for the gates. She was going to be free! She was going to be away from these monsters who were using her as a punchbag. She thought of how she would tell the police what they had done and they would go to prison. Of course, when you are a sprightly seven-year-old, anything is possible! Lesley started to walk the way she knew, the way that would take her to Glasgow, where the overnight coaches departed from. Lesley was sure someone would take pity on her and get her onto the coach south, to the sanctuary of her grandparents.

She walked and walked. It was a cool evening, so it was easy for Lesley to walk faster to keep warm. Lesley had no food, she hadn't eaten since her school dinner and she was hungry, but determination drove her on. It started to get dark and Lesley was tired now. She was looking at the derelict buildings, shells of tenement buildings that were no longer occupied. The tenants had long since been rehoused in tower blocks that blighted the landscape. Lesley was tempted to climb into one of the buildings, but she had heard terrible stories of them collapsing in the night, or tramps going in there and killing people. She decided she wasn't brave enough to take the chance so she kept going.

Just as she was starting to despair, she saw a policeman coming towards her. Lesley thought that if she told him of her predicament, he would take her somewhere safe, far from Pam and Nuri. 'Hello, little girl. What's your name?' He was a tall, thick-set man, PC Baker. He had been in the police force for many years and wasn't far off retirement now. He had seen many waifs and strays on the streets over the long span of his career. He knew that children never run away for no reason; after all, the streets are dangerous for a young child away from its home. There were many varied reasons for running away. Some ran away because of cruelty at home; some had parents who were drug addicts or drunks; some children had parents who had separated and the child wanted to be with the other parent. This little girl looked very sad and completely lost.

'Please, sir, my name's Lesley,' she said.

PC Baker squatted down to talk to her. 'And where might you be going tonight?' he asked her.

Lesley felt uneasy. She wanted to pour her heart out to this nice policeman; after all, the police were there to help children, weren't they?

'Please sir, I'm hungry,' Lesley said.

'Come on then, how about I buy you some chips and you tell me why you're not at home, where you should be?'

'Alright,' Lesley replied. She'd have done anything for a bit of food at that moment.

PC Baker took her to the local chip shop and bought her some chips. As they walked, Lesley explained her life story to him from the beginning.

'So you see, sir,' she said, 'I just want to be safe. I want to go back to my grandma and granddad because I know they will look after me properly and not beat me every day.'

PC Baker didn't much like the sound of what this little one was telling him but he knew she wasn't going to get to Reading any time soon, and definitely not tonight. In any case, his shift was about to end, so it would be better if he could make Lesley go home. He persuaded Lesley that as it was cold, dark and due to rain, and no little girl was going to be safe on the streets, it would be better if she went home tonight. Lesley had realised by now that she was on a losing wicket, so reluctantly she agreed to go home with PC Baker.

As the police car pulled up outside the house, PC Baker was immediately struck by how frightened Lesley seemed and how she shook with fear and hung her head as she trudged up the drive behind him. He thought that this big house was hiding some terrible secrets but that the little girl was better off in a warm bed than on the street where she would always be in danger.

Pam opened the door and glared at Lesley. 'Thank you so much for bringing her home. We were so worried,' she said to PC Baker in that sickly voice Lesley had come to know so well. Lesley knew that was a complete lie but stood quietly.

'You're welcome, Mrs. Always pleased to help. I bid you goodnight.' PC Baker turned to walk away and looked back at Lesley. Tears were rolling down her cheeks and she looked terrified. He forced himself to walk away with a heavy heart.

The minute the door clicked shut, Lesley knew she was in for a severe beating. Sure enough, she was dragged into the piano room by her hair and thrown on the floor in a heap. She was sobbing now and Nuri was stood over her, riding crop at the ready. Pam spoke. 'You, young lady, are an ungrateful little bitch! We gave you a home when nobody wanted you and this is how you repay us. You must pay the price for your selfishness. Any more of this nonsense and we'll send you to the workhouse. Nuri, deal with her.'

Lesley didn't know what the workhouse was, but it had to be better than living here, she was sure of that.

Chapter 6

Lesley's Worst Nightmare Comes True

In 1966, Lesley once more noticed that Pam was getting fat and wearing her tent dresses. This time she rightly worked out that another baby was on the way. Pam's parents came from Harrogate to stay to look after Lucy while Pam seemed to be ill and take to her bed much more than she ever had done with Lucy. Then one cold day in December 1966, Lesley returned home from school to find Pam gone. She had been taken into hospital to have the child. This time she gave birth to a son, John. All was not well with mother or baby, and Lesley secretly wished they would both die, in the hope that she would be returned to her grandparents. After what seemed like an eternity, Pam came home. Christmas had come and gone, relatives had come and gone, but still Pam remained unwell. Lesley really hoped that, now Pam and Nuri had two children of their own, she might be allowed to leave this awful house. No such luck.

Instead, they used Lesley as a servant. Fetch this, take that, hang the washing out, bring it in. Feed the dogs, walk the dogs, put the rubbish out, do the vacuuming and polishing. Lesley was exhausted! Going to school was bad enough, but to have to do all these extra duties as well was just plain cheeky!

Lesley grew to resent the children. Lucy was never scolded; she made a mess everywhere and Lesley had to clean it up. As she got older, she would grow to hate both children. They would break things or cause trouble and blame Lesley for it, as did Simon. It seemed she was everyone's scapegoat and the beatings came thick and fast.

Many, many times, Lesley wondered what had become of her mother and her grandparents. They didn't write, they didn't phone and they didn't send presents or cards. Lesley couldn't understand it, nor could she believe the story about her father's death in such strange circumstances. There were numerous occasions when she wished she could ask someone, but who? She didn't even have her grandparents' address any more. All links to her past had been erased by Pam and Nuri, with the threat of a beating if she tried to find out anything about her true family. Lesley thought they were very cruel. Her friends at school all had lovely parents who came and met them at the gates, bought them sweets to eat on the way home and were eager to hear about their day. Lesley was all alone each day as she walked home. She had no money to buy sweets from the shops like her friends and she was never allowed to go to their houses for tea, like the other children. Each parents' evening at school, Lesley would eagerly await Pam and Nuri's return from their visit, hoping for praise and perhaps a chocolate bar as a reward. Instead, she was rewarded with a beating. No matter how hard she worked, it was never good enough. Even when she was top of the class, it wasn't good enough for them. The mark could have been higher, the work could have been neater. Every criticism, but never praise.

Lesley was about to have the worst experience of her whole school life. The day started off like any other day, but as the morning wore on, Lesley started to feel her stomach gurgling and she had cramps in her tummy.

Lunchtime came and as usual, she and her classmates all raced into the dining hall. However, Lesley felt a bit off-colour, so she picked at her meal, before running off to the toilet in a great hurry. The bell went for the afternoon session and all the children filed into the classroom. Lesley was eight years old now. She didn't much like this year's teacher, Miss Welch. She was a scary woman with dark hair and very sharp features and Lesley was terrified of her. In fact, she was as terrified of Miss Welch as she was of Pam! This was not going to be a good year for the little girl.

Halfway through the afternoon, Lesley's stomach started to gurgle again. Fearing the inevitable, she put her hand up. 'Please, miss. Please, miss.'

Miss Welch was not amused. 'What do you want?' she barked at Lesley.

'Please, miss, my tummy, I need the toilet, now.'

Miss Welch glared at her. 'You'll have to wait till break time,' she said indifferently.

Lesley's voice took on a new urgency. 'But miss, I need the toilet.'

Miss Welch was irritated now. 'You should have gone at lunchtime, then!' she barked. Lesley was now in dire need of the toilet and she clenched the cheeks of her bottom as tightly as she could, but to no avail. There was a great explosion as her stomach contents emptied onto the floor of the classroom.

Miss Welch was incandescent with rage now. 'What on earth?!' she shouted. 'What's that smell?'

Some of the children were laughing, they found Lesley's humiliation amusing. Lesley was crying now, her underwear soiled, her dignity undone. Miss Welch ordered Lesley out of the classroom into the toilets. She evacuated the children from the class into the school hall, then summoned the janitor to come and clear up the mess. Poor Lesley tried desperately to clean some of the mess from her little bottom and her underwear, but did not have much luck. She was afraid of Miss Welch, but she was more petrified at the prospect of trying to explain to Pam what had happened. What would she say? What would the punishment be? Lesley had never been so afraid. She ran all the way home from school and raced upstairs to the bathroom. She tried desperately to clean herself and her underwear. She had done her best but she didn't smell great and as the house warmed up, the smell got stronger.

She was too afraid to tell Pam what had happened, so she sat quietly, until suddenly Pam said, 'What is that dreadful smell?'

Lesley cleared her throat and whispered, 'I had an accident at school.' The reaction she got was as if she had set off an atomic bomb! Lesley started to cry as she explained to Pam, 'I tried to ask the teacher if I could go to the toilet, but she wouldn't let me. I had an accident. I've tried to clean it up.'

Pam was purple in the face now. 'Get up to the bloody bathroom, girl,' she yelled. Lesley raced up the stairs as fast as her little legs would carry her. Pam was right behind her. Oh no, this was going to end badly. 'Get in the bath,' Pam barked. Lesley took her slippers off and climbed into the bath. 'Take your clothes off and put them in the bath,' Pam ordered her. Lesley did as she was told, wondering what terrible thing would happen next. Pam lifted the shower head out of its cradle. 'Right, here we go,' she said. Lesley gasped as the freezing cold water cascaded down her tiny body, making her yell. As Pam washed Lesley down as roughly as she could, she planted fists wherever they landed, on her head, on her back, around her private parts.

'Dirty bitch! Dirty bitch!' she kept saying, as Lesley tried to dodge another punch.

When Pam was satisfied that Lesley was clean enough, she instructed her to climb out of the bath. 'Stand by the basin,' Pam ordered. Lesley did as she was told, shivering with cold and fear. She cursed Miss Welch for putting her through this ordeal, and she cursed Pam for being such a monster. Lesley would never forget this day in all her life-time. She stood by the basin, waiting for something to happen – and it certainly did. Pam grabbed the soiled underpants, and proceeded to rub the faeces into Lesley's mouth, making her gag. Lesley tried to pull away, but Pam had a firm hold of her hair and she held Lesley still as she stuffed the soiled underpants into her mouth over and over again.

'This will teach you a lesson!' she shouted as Lesley was sick in the sink again. Lesley was choking, trying to avoid the stinking underwear and be sick and cry at the same time. Then the pants were thrown back in the bath. Lesley almost breathed a sigh of relief, but before she had chance to do so, a bar of carbolic soap was stuffed into her mouth, which was just as bad as the underpants but in a different way. Lesley gagged again as her mouth bubbled with the soap. She wished she was dead, then she wouldn't have to go through such a dreadful ordeal ever again.

Finally, Pam had had enough of her sadistic game and Lesley was allowed to clean her teeth. She was sent straight to bed without any food or a drink, but she didn't mind. She just wanted to be away from this situation. The sad, forlorn little body climbed into bed. When she was sure Pam and Nuri were in bed that night, Lesley slowly removed the cord from her dressing gown. She carefully tied one end round the catch on the sash window, then she gently tied the other end round her neck and pulled. The noose tightened and Lesley started to see stars. She had heard that you could die doing this, but she wasn't sure how to do it quickly and painlessly. She didn't fancy gasping for air for hours on end. As she started to feel faint, she panicked and changed her mind. At least she knew this was an option, if she chose to do it for real. Lesley would wish she was dead many more times during the next few years of her life.

Her unfortunate accident was never mentioned in the class again, but a few of the children took great delight in reminding her about the day she messed herself in class. Thankfully, children are easily distracted and they soon found something else to occupy their time. Lesley decided that she hated Miss Welch and for the rest of that year did everything she possibly could to irritate her.

This ploy backfired towards the end of the school year. Lesley always used to sit at the back of the classroom, as far away from Miss Welch as she could get. One day, Miss Welch told the class that they would be learning multiplication. Sitting at the back, Lesley carefully wrote all the numbers down and followed the instructions on how to complete the sums. 'Right, then. Swap your books with the person sitting next to you,' Miss Welch barked. She read each answer out and Lesley duly put a tick or a cross next to the sums in the book in front of her.

The girl next to her handed her book back and said quietly, 'You've got them all wrong.' Lesley was a bit taken aback. She thought she had understood the instructions Miss Welch had given the class. Miss Welch asked the whole class to stand up. 'When I call out the number of sums you have correct, sit down,' she instructed. She started to count, 'One, two, three, four'. A few of the children sat down. She carried on, 'five, six, seven eight, nine, ten'. Lesley was the only child still standing. 'How many did you get right?' Miss Welch asked her.

'None, miss,' Lesley said.

There were sniggers all around the classroom. Lesley wished the answers could magically all be right so that she didn't get into trouble. 'Come to the front and bring your answers with you,' Miss Welch shouted. Lesley took her exercise book and went to the front. Miss Welch was annoyed. 'These numbers are not the numbers on the board,' she said. 'Where did you get these numbers from?' Lesley was perplexed. She had written down what was written on the board, but now she was at the front the numbers had all changed, as if by magic!

Lesley felt humiliated, again. Miss Welch told her to go back to her seat and follow the next set of numbers more carefully. Lesley sat down and looked at the girl next to her, shrugging her shoulders in confusion. Once again she wrote the next set of numbers down and once again they were all wrong. Miss Welch was now really angry and Lesley was really scared.

'What is the matter with you, girl?' the teacher barked at her.

'But miss, I wrote down the numbers you gave out,' Lesley said. Miss Welch didn't like this girl. She seemed to be afraid of her own shadow, yet she had intelligence. Miss Welch felt uneasy. She didn't want the class to think she was weak and would give in to the girl, who quite obviously had deliberately written down the wrong numbers twice over!

Unfortunately, in Scotland in the 1960s, corporal punishment was considered acceptable. Lesley was about to find this out, the hard way. Miss Welch summoned her to the desk and said to the class, 'This is what will happen if anyone tries to be clever and make me look stupid, do you all understand?'

There was a murmur of 'Yes, miss,' around the room. Miss Welch produced the belt from her desk. It was a long leather strip with two narrower strips at one end. It reminded Lesley of the riding crop she was so used to.

'Hold your hands out,' Miss Welch ordered. Lesley did as was told and closed her eyes as she waited for the hard leather to hit her already sore, bruised little hands. Thwack! The leather hit her hand and she jumped. Thwack! The belt came down a second time. Lesley kept her composure. This bitch wasn't going to get the better of her. Besides, the beatings she was used to were far worse than this. Lesley returned to her seat, grinning at the children on her way. She would save her tears for later, when she was alone in her bedroom.

However, knowing that she was in the right, Lesley thought it prudent to tell Pam what had happened. Someone from school always seemed to be telling tales about Lesley, so best she confess now. Over the evening meal, she explained how she had written the numbers down that were on the board but she had been punished because she had written down the wrong numbers. Lesley said how sure she was that the numbers on the board were not the same ones she had seen when she went to the front of the class. Pam came into school the following afternoon, just as the last bell had gone. Pam told Lesley to sit at the back of the class, while she wrote some numbers on the board, much to the amusement of Miss Welch. Pam said to Lesley, 'Bring me your book and show me what you have written.' Lesley took her book to the front and, sure enough, she had written down totally different numbers to the ones on the board.

'Go and sit in the classroom, and tell me when the numbers on the board start to look different,' Pam said. Lesley walked slowly back, row one, row two, row three, then as she watched, as if by magic, the numbers started to look different.

'Here,' Lesley said. 'The numbers look different now.' Pam turned to Miss Welch and shouted at her, 'You stupid woman! She can't see! The girl is short-sighted! You punished her for nothing.'

Miss Welch was gobsmacked! She didn't like Lesley anyway, and now her parent was here telling her off. Pam quickly marched Lesley out of the classroom. 'We need to get your eyes tested.'

Whilst she waited for her eye appointment, Lesley always sat at the front of the class, lest she should fall prey to Miss Welch's well-known temper again. After a week or two, an appointment came through and Lesley was taken to the eye clinic for her eye examination. The eye clinic was in a portable building attached to the local ante-natal clinic. It was a long building, with very yellow lights and equally yellow walls, although Lesley couldn't work out if that was simply because of the lighting. There were several rooms and every so often a nurse would come out and call a name. At last it was Lesley's turn to go in. Lesley was bored by now, but she thought it was better to be here than to be in the classroom, with Miss Welch bellowing at the class!

The optician was a funny little man; he reminded Lesley of one of Santa's elves. He beckoned Lesley to his desk, which was covered in paperwork. 'Now then, young lady, I understand you're having a bit of trouble at school,' the man said.

Lesley turned to Pam, who nodded gently and said, 'Tell the nice man what happened to you at school.'

Lesley took a deep breath and said, 'Well, sir, I was sat at the back of the class. The teacher wrote some numbers on the board and I wrote them down, but they were the wrong numbers, sir. I got the belt because I wrote them down wrong.'

The optician's expression softened. 'So, what you are telling me is, you wrote down what you thought you saw, but it was all wrong?'

'Yes, sir,' Lesley replied.

The optician smiled. 'Don't worry. We'll have you sorted out in no time at all.'

'Thank you, sir,' Lesley said.

The optician explained that he would put some big heavy metal glasses on Lesley's head. Lesley was glad there wasn't a mirror anywhere near; she thought she must look like a freak with this frame on.

The optician continued, 'Now I will show you some letters and you must tell me what you see. Then I will fit different lenses into the frames and you can tell me if it makes the letters clearer or more blurred. Do you think you can do that?' Lesley nodded and the tests began.

Lesley started to giggle as the lenses clanked into the frame, but a dig in her arm from Pam's claw-like nails reminded her that this was a serious business. The eye examination seemed to take an eternity and Lesley was starting to wish she could go back to school. Suddenly, the optician was finished and the bright fluorescent lights were switched back on, which made Lesley blink in pain.

The optician removed the big heavy frames containing the final lens prescription. He turned to Pam. 'I really don't know how this child has managed to get to school without getting run over,' he said. 'She is very short-sighted and needs spectacles straight away.'

Pam looked a bit stern. 'How much is that going to cost?' The irritation in her voice was obvious.

'If Lesley has National Health Service frames, her spectacles will be free,' he explained. He handed the prescription for Lesley's spectacles to Pam.

'Come on, then,' Pam said as she pushed Lesley out through the door.

'Thank you, sir,' Lesley called back as she went out through the door.

Lesley was taken home for lunch, then Pam walked her back to school. All her friends were very curious as to what had happened and what her spectacles would look like. Lesley explained about the optician and how he had tested her eyes and how she had been made to sit in the dark looking at letters on a funny chart. Lesley couldn't wait to tell Miss Welch that she was indeed very short-sighted and that Miss Welch had punished her for nothing.

Eventually, Pam and Nuri took Lesley to the only optician in the town. The shop was very small and it smelt of damp. The assistant was friendly and Lesley was excited at the prospect of finally getting her spectacles. Lesley was expecting to have some pretty frames. There were frames with flowers on and frames that flicked up at the edges. There were blue ones, pink ones, tortoiseshell ones, so much choice, Lesley thought as she looked along the shelf.

Her excitement was short-lived. Pam asked the optician to bring the National Health Service frames for Lesley to look at. To Lesley's horror, he only brought two frames out. One was pink, the other blue. They were horrid! The frames were perfectly round, like bicycle wheels, with thin wires that held them on the ears. Lesley hated them! Her eyes were drawn to a pretty pair on the shelf: pink with pretty little flowers in the design. The frame on the desk in front of her was barely pink; the colour was a non-colour; they might as well have been invisible.

Lesley looked at Pam. 'Can't I have those, please?' she asked her, pointing to the pretty frames with the little flowers on.

'They're far too expensive!' Pam retorted. 'Besides, you'll drop them and break them in no time. You'll have what you're given and be grateful.' Lesley knew better than to try and argue with Pam. She looked at the optician. 'Please may I have the blue ones, sir?' she asked.

Pam stepped forward. 'Pink, girl! Pink! Pink is for girls!'

Lesley thought for a moment. If she was going to have these ridiculous spectacles, she would want them in a colour she liked. 'Please let me have the blue ones,' she begged Pam. Lesley held the little frames in her hands, secretly wishing they would suddenly disappear in a puff of smoke, so that she could have her pretty pair.

'Very well,' Pam said, 'but just remember, you can't change your mind once they're ready.'

'I won't,' Lesley replied. Two weeks later, the spectacles were ready for collection. Lesley was once more taken to the optician's shop to collect her glasses.

'Ah, good to see you again, young lady,' the optician said.

Lesley had mixed feelings about having to wear the ridiculous frames she had been forced to have. She hated the frames, but at least she would be able to see properly. The optician brought out her spectacles and Lesley put them on. She thought they didn't look too bad and best of all, she could see everything around her very clearly. She looked out through the shop window. She could see all the way up Brandon Parade. What a revelation! Lesley laughed with glee at the new world which had opened up to her.

'Well? What do you think?' the optician asked her.

'They're great, sir. I can see everything so clearly now!'

The optician gave Pam the case for the spectacles and a guide as to how they should be cleaned. Pam thanked the optician and they left the shop. Over the rest of the weekend, Lesley surveyed her new found world. She could see everything so clearly and she could see things a long way off, which before had just been a blur. This was fun!

Monday morning came around and Lesley thought her friends would love her new look, but she was to be very disappointed. Children can be so cruel! The chants of 'Specky Four Eyes' and 'Yo Biggles' were everywhere. Lesley desperately tried to find a corner of the playground to hide in, but wherever she went, the children would find her and taunt her about the glasses. Lesley made sure she was the last one to queue after break, hoping the children wouldn't notice she was there, but once more, they were taunting her, whispering so that the teachers couldn't hear. Luckily, children get bored easily, so after a couple of weeks Lesley's spectacles were no longer the gossip of the moment, much to her relief.

Chapter 7

For Once, Lesley Gets the Upper Hand

—◦⊙◦—

Nuri worked at the newest and best place to be employed at that time, the big Honeywell factory in Newhouse. Each morning he had to leave early to catch the bus to work. He was a diligent and eager worker, involved in the design of the first-generation computers. His employers were so impressed with his work that they offered him a job in the United States, for one year. Pam was not happy about being left on her own, but she accepted that it would improve their financial situation and Nuri's standing with his employers. He flew out to America in July 1968, leaving Pam in charge of the household. Lesley, by now aged eight, was nervous about this. Would she be beaten more regularly now that Pam was stressed about her husband being abroad? Lesley was very careful to toe the line to avoid a beating.

The long summer holidays came around again and Pam decided that a family holiday would be a good idea and enlisted Lillian and Harry as chauffeurs. The packing of the car seemed to take forever, but eventually Lillian, Harry, Pam, Lesley, Lucy and John were all crammed into Harry's tiny Hillman Minx estate car and they set off. As Simon was older and Nuri's parents thought he was wonderful, the decision was made that he would stay behind and they would supervise him. The holiday was going to be in the Orkney Islands. Lesley had never been there, and it seemed a long way away, but she allowed herself to feel just a little bit excited.

Pam and her parents did not get on particularly well. Pam would speak to her parents as if she was the parent, which Lillian found very annoying and let her daughter know in no uncertain terms. The journey was hot, they were frequently lost and the bickering between Pam and her parents became very tiresome.

They reached Aberdeen that night, where they stayed in a small hotel. The next morning the little party set out for Thurso, to catch the ferry across to the Orkney Islands. Pam argued constantly with her parents about whether the children should be allowed on deck, whether they should eat in the restaurant, whether they should do a food shop on the mainland or on the Orkneys. In fact, Lesley wished they would shut up as the constant arguments were driving her mad!

At last the grumpy grandparents and a very stressed Pam boarded the ferry with Lesley. Lesley rushed to the side; she loved the sound of the waves lapping at the boat and the seagulls shrieking overhead as the fishermen threw their scraps back into the sea. The salt water speckled Lesley's lips and she smiled, this felt wonderful. Suddenly she was aware of an iron grip on her shoulder. Pam guided her towards the entrance into the decks and she was whisked off to have a meal before they reached Orkney. The journey wasn't as long as she would have liked, but Lesley didn't care; she was happy being on the water. As Orkney drew nearer, Lesley was amazed at how unpopulated it seemed to be. She had only ever known busy towns and cities, so this was a whole new experience.

The little party was booked into a guest house on a working farm, not far from Stromness. Pam wanted to get unpacked but Lesley was far more interested in all the farm animals and the farmer's dog, which followed her everywhere. The grandparents were, by this time, heartily sick of the sight and sound of their daughter, so they retreated to their allocated bedroom to unpack and rest after the journey. Lesley asked permission to have a wander round. 'I suppose it won't hurt,' Pam said. 'Make sure you're back here for seven o'clock for a bath and bed.'

Lesley ran out of the tiny farmhouse. The fresh breeze blew her hair and she could taste the salt in the air as she ran. The farmer's dog, a beautiful collie, followed her around, more like a sheep than a dog, Lesley thought. The farm ended at the sea. Lesley walked down to the waterfront and gazed up and down the inlet. As she did so, a tiny fishing vessel passed by and blew the horn as it passed, at which point the farmer's wife appeared and waved back. 'That's my son in that boat,' she said. 'He'll be bringing the crabs back for me to shell. He catches them fresh every day so if you see that boat, you know we've got crabs coming ashore.' Lesley was fascinated. She had never seen a live crab, only pictures of them in books.

The next few days were spent wandering the islands. They visited Scapa Flow and saw some of the shipwrecked boats strewn along the coastline. There was an ancient Viking village too; Lesley was amazed to think that there was a settlement here long before she was around. She wondered how the settlers had survived the vicious winds and the power of the sea on these desolate islands. All too soon it was time to head back to the farmhouse for her bath, but Lesley felt happy as she skipped along the path. She slept very well that night.

The next morning, breakfast was served in the dining room. There was cereal, toast, fruit juice, fried egg and bacon with beans and as much tea and coffee as you could drink. Lesley was amazed. This was a feast compared to the one slice of toast she was allowed at the house in Motherwell. Lesley tried some orange juice. She liked the taste so asked if she could have another glass.

Pam scowled at her. 'No you can't. Don't be a pig,' she growled. Then Lesley asked if she could have a fried breakfast. Again Pam pulled a face. 'Since when do you eat bacon and egg?' she moaned.

At this point, Lillian intervened. 'For goodness' sake, let the child have what she wants. It will be hours before we get any lunch. Stop moaning at her every time she opens her mouth!' Lesley smiled at Lillian.

Pam glared at her mother, then at Lesley. 'Very well, but don't come crying to me if you feel sick later,' she said.

Lesley polished off her breakfast and went upstairs to get her coat and shoes, ready for the day out.

'You might want your swimsuit today,' Lillian said. 'We're going to the beach.'

Now Lesley was excited. The beach! She couldn't remember the last time she had been on sand or felt the waves lapping at her toes. Lesley grabbed her swimsuit and towel and headed for the door. Although this was proving to be a reasonable holiday, it made Lesley realise that she hadn't heard from her mum or her grandparents in so long. She felt very sad to think they had just abandoned her and now she felt sad that they weren't here to see her enjoying her very first holiday.

The farmer's wife sensed the fear in the little girl. Every time her mother came near, the little girl would flinch, as if expecting to be slapped. The farmer's wife was a mother herself and she was concerned. However, she knew better than to say anything. Comments made out of place could ruin a business, and goodness' knows it was tough enough to make a living on these islands. If it weren't for the tourists, many a farm would have folded long since. The farmer's wife put an arm round Lesley. 'When you come back from the beach, would you like to see me cook the crabs?' she asked.

Lesley looked at Pam nervously. She knew better than to agree to anything without first asking permission. 'Yes, that will be fine,' Pam said. 'I'm sure Lesley would love to see how you prepare the crabs for the pot.'

They set off for the beach. For once there was no bickering or arguments. All of them were eager to see the beautiful coastline and to feel the sand between their toes. They reached a little inlet and Granddad Harry pulled into a parking space. 'It should be easy to carry the blankets and picnic across the sand dunes from here,' he said. Each of them grabbed something from out of the boot of the car and headed over the sand dunes.

As Lesley got to the top of the dune, she gasped in amazement. There was the most beautiful beach she had ever seen. The sand was clean and laid like a sheet of gold before her, while the crystal-clear water was like diamonds shimmering in the sunlight. Lesley thought that this must be paradise, then a cold gust of wind caught her and she remembered that this was the north of Scotland, not the Caribbean!

The day on the beach was wonderful. Lesley made sand-castles for Lucy and John and paddled with them in the sea. She even felt brave enough to go swimming and snorkelling around one of the shipwrecks, which was at the end of the beach. When it got too cold to remain, Pam suggested they go and find a tearoom, which was met with agreement by all.

When they got back to the farmhouse, the adults and younger children went for a walk. Lesley headed for the kitchen, remembering that she had been promised a lesson in how to cook and shell crabs. The farmer's wife was sat at a big oak table in her cosy kitchen. The cooker wasn't a cooker as Lesley knew it, so the farmer's wife showed her all the compartments and explained that this provided heat and warmth for the farm workers and her fisherman son. 'Right then, young lady, we need to find you an apron. Can't be spoiling them posh clothes you're wearing,' the farmer's wife said kindly. She went to a big chest of drawers in the corner and started rummaging through it. Lesley was bemused by all the things that were crammed in the drawer. It seemed to have everything in it except for an apron! Eventually, the farmer's wife found a spare apron and gave it to Lesley to put on.

The farmer's wife observed quietly as Lesley's little hands shook with nerves as she tried to fasten the bow at the back of the apron. 'Come here, dear,' she said. 'Let me do it for you. Don't be afraid of me – I won't hurt you.'

The little girl looked as if she might burst into tears, then she smiled and said, 'Thank you. I'm not used to people being nice to me.'

'No need to state the obvious, little one,' the farmer's wife replied. 'I've seen the fear in your eyes whenever your mother is near.'

Lesley snorted. 'She's not my mother. She's nothing like my mother,' the little girl said defiantly. 'My mother is kind and gentle and never beats me.'

The older woman was disturbed by this outburst. Whatever had happened in this child's life had clearly upset her greatly.

The farmer's wife picked up a crab and it clacked its

pincers together furiously. Lesley let out a scream! She'd never seen one of these things close up before and she had no idea they had big claws like that. The farmer's wife laughed. 'You've never seen a live crab before, I take it?' Lesley shook her head. 'Watch this,' the farmer's wife said. She picked up the crab and threw it into a pan of boiling water. Lesley waited, then screamed in horror as she realised that the noise she was now hearing was the sound of the crab being boiled alive. Lesley was horrified. This seemed so barbaric.

The farmer's wife said, 'Don't worry, dear. He'll be gone in an instant, and then we'll shell it and you can try the meat. Have you ever had crab meat?' Lesley shook her head again. 'For goodness' sake, little one, are you not capable of speaking now?'

Lesley smiled. 'Yes, but I wasn't expecting that to happen. I thought you hit them with a hammer or something!' The farmer's wife laughed heartily. She'd heard it all now!

'Wait till I tell my boys,' she said in between shrieks of laughter. 'They'll be amused alright.' When the crab was cooked, the farmer's wife took it out of the pan and laid it on a wooden slab on the table. She expertly broke off the claws, showing Lesley which bits were edible and which meat was poisonous. Lesley tried some of the white meat. To her utter amazement, it was the most succulent, tasty meat she had ever eaten.

'It's gorgeous!' she said to the farmer's wife.

'I know, girl. My son caught it, so of course it's delicious.'

The rest of the holiday passed with not too many unpleasant incidents. Pam had to behave with her parents around. She seemed to think twice before shouting at

Lesley, although a deft punch here and there was still administered slyly. Soon the holiday was over and it was time to return home. The trip back to Motherwell was thankfully, a much more peaceful affair, without all the bickering there had been on the journey there.

Soon it was Lesley's ninth birthday, which passed, like all the others, with no fuss, no party, just the grumpy grandparents from down the road, and Pam. Nuri was going to and from America with his company, so for long periods of time Pam was in sole charge of the household. Lesley was getting older and wiser and her hatred of Pam and Nuri and their horrible house was growing. If Pam threatened her with a beating, Lesley would feign illness and pretend to retch, as if she was going to be sick. Pam soon changed her mind and the moment passed.

Lesley asked her friends at school what their parents expected them to do in the house. Some of her friends were not expected to do anything to help, whilst others were asked to help now and again. There was no compulsion to do gardening, or cleaning, or cleaning shoes for the family. None of them had to spend the school holidays cleaning, gardening or painting like Lesley did. Lesley's friends were horrified when she explained that she had to do all the cleaning, all the gardening and she had to clean all the shoes every night, otherwise she would be beaten. She had even been asked to go and do some painting at Nuri's parents' house down the road. Some of the children thought she was making these stories up to gain friends and they also beat her around. Lesley, being thoroughly fed up by now of beatings, fought back. Even the school hard nuts learnt not to pick on her.

Lesley decided that she was not going to be the house servant. She dusted, but only where the dust showed. She wiped the shoes with a cloth instead of applying polish. She cleaned the skirting boards, but only where it showed. She put the dishes away in the kitchen before they were dry. She was sick of drying up every night. Lesley felt better, she thought that if her friends could go out and play all day, then she should also be doing the same, not enslaved in this prison of a house. It worked very well, until one day, Lesley had been told off yet again. In a particularly spiteful mood, she decided to wipe the shoes in the corner of Pam's coat. Unfortunately, the grumpy grandparents from down the road opened the door just as she was doing this.

'What do you think you're doing?' Grumpy Granddad demanded.

'Nothing,' Lesley said defiantly.

'Doesn't look like nothing to me,' he growled.

Lesley was summoned to the dining room, where the grumpy grandparents and Pam were sitting. Pam demanded to know what was going on and Grumpy Granddad explained what he had seen. Pam shouted at Lesley, then she shouted at Grumpy Granddad that as Nuri was away in America, he would need to administer the riding crop beating. Lesley hated them. She hated Pam and Nuri, she hated Nuri's parents ... in fact, she hated everybody! Grumpy Granddad took Lesley to her room, where the riding crop was used to give her a sound beating. Lesley waited for him to go back downstairs, then sat on her bed and prayed to God that they would all die before she killed them. Years later, Lesley would discover that Grumpy Granddad was in fact, her lovely, sweet granddad's brother. To compound the situation, Grumpy Grandma was her beautiful, sweet-natured grandma's sister. What a very strange family she had been born into. No wonder they were all weird!

After six months, Nuri came home to spend some time with Pam. She was sweetness and light itself, so pleased to see him. It made Lesley sick. She carried on as usual, doing half the housework, but as she was only nine, she didn't see why she should have to do all the cleaning. She thought Pam was a lazy bitch. Then, one day, Pam was in a very bad mood and shouted at Nuri all day. Lesley had no idea what was wrong. Mealtimes were spent in total silence, which was unusual as they had been parted for six months. Lesley was treading very carefully.

Pam was going upstairs when Lesley heard her name being called, or rather, shouted. She went to the bottom of the stairs. 'Come here at once!' Pam shouted. Lesley slowly climbed the stairs to where Pam was standing. 'What's this?' Pam shouted.

'What?' Lesley asked cheekily.

'It's dust, girl. Dust!' Pam was fuming.

Lesley was fed up with being a servant. She had been slaving after these people for four years and now she really had just about had enough. 'So?' Lesley said.

Pam couldn't believe the insolence of this child. She grabbed Lesley by the hair and marched her to the lounge. Nuri was sitting reading quietly. He looked up at Pam wearily. 'What now?' he asked her.

'This little bitch has only been doing half the cleaning! She thinks I'm stupid! I'm not having it!' she shouted.

Nuri turned to Lesley and asked, 'What have you got to say for yourself?' Lesley was full of spite and hatred for these two. She would say her piece and hang the consequences. 'None of my friends have to do chores! Their parents don't make them do cleaning and gardening and washing and drying up and changing beds!' Lesley was so furious she was almost spitting the words at them.

Now Pam was angry. 'You ungracious, ungrateful little bitch!' she yelled. 'If it wasn't for us, you'd be out on the street, you and that no good mother of yours!'

Lesley opened her mouth, not thinking what was coming out. 'My mother never beat me, never made me a slave in the house. She was a good mum, unlike you two, who beat me every day. That's just not normal!' Lesley knew she was in trouble now.

Unfortunately, as Pam and Nuri had argued so much already that day, Lesley was the scapegoat. Out came the riding crop and the beating began. However, Lesley was not going to give in easily either and as Nuri was beating her, she stood up. Pam went to punch her back to the bed but caught her eye instead, instantly smashing the glass lenses of her spectacles into her eyes.

Nuri started to shout at Pam, 'What have you done? She could go blind and if we can't get the glass out, we'll have to take her to hospital! Oh God, then they'll find out we've been beating her and see all the bruises … We could go to prison! You stupid woman!' Nuri was hysterical now.

Lesley smirked to herself, wondering how they were going to get out of this predicament. Then her eyes started to hurt and realising the lenses were made of glass, Lesley started to yell, 'I can't see, I can't see!' Pam grabbed her by the arm and tried to get her to the bathroom, but Lesley couldn't see at all and was frightened to move her eyes in case the glass dug into her eyeball.

Nuri was getting worried now. 'Come on, Lesley. Take my arm and I will guide you to the bathroom.' Lesley allowed herself to be guided slowly to the bathroom, terrified that if she fell, the glass might penetrate her eye and she would go blind. She wanted to scream but knew that this could push Pam over the edge and she could get another beating.

Several eye baths later, they asked, 'Can you see now?'

Lesley looked around, her eyes stinging from the water and the scratches from the glass. 'I can see a bit, but I won't be able to see the blackboard,' she said. Pam was worried. She knew that sending the girl to school minus her spec-tacles was a risky tactic. What if the girl happened to tell someone what had happened and they believed her? What would happen to her teaching career and to Nuri's high-flying engineering design career? Pam thought for a moment, then softened her tone as she spoke to Lesley, who was by now cowering in the corner of the room, just in case they decided they hadn't beaten her enough.

'Tell you what,' Pam said. 'How about we go to the opticians tomorrow and you choose some new glasses. I will let you choose whichever ones you want, as long as you don't tell anyone what really happened tonight.' Lesley had always known that Pam was a cold, sadistic, cruel bitch, but for once she smiled to herself. This time Lesley would have Pam just where she wanted her. Now she would have the spectacles she wanted. She knew Pam couldn't argue with her; Lesley had the upper hand. If she told anyone what really happened … She smiled as she thought of the chaos she could bring to their cosy world.

The optician was surprised to see the little girl back quite so soon. Pam said, 'Lesley had an accident and dropped her spectacles outside, so we thought we would replace them with those pretty ones she wanted.' The optician couldn't do enough, fawning over Lesley as he thought of the profit he would gain from selling them the most expensive frames in the shop. Lesley ran to the pretty frames she had seen and been denied on her previous visit.

Pam glowered at her. 'They're far too expensive,' she hissed.

Lesley wasn't going to be deterred this time. She handed the pretty frames to the optician and said, 'Do you know how my glasses really got broken?' The optician was intrigued and got the feeling that this little girl was terrified of Pam. He wondered whether some incident might have resulted in the breakage, so soon after the original purchase.

'Go on, then,' the optician said, 'tell me what happened.'

Before Lesley could open her mouth to reply, Pam interrupted sternly. 'Come along, the optician doesn't have time to listen to your ramblings,' she said. 'Besides, I have other errands to do today.' Pam turned to the optician. 'Please can you measure her up for those pretty frames? She won't give up till I let her have them.'

Lesley was now grinning from ear to ear. Under her breath she was thinking, 'I won, bitch! I won!'

After a week of struggling at school and telling endless lies about how her glasses got broken, Lesley finally had her new pair. Even though she now had new spectacles, the beatings didn't stop. Each time she was beaten, Lesley was told to remove her spectacles 'for your own safety'. How ironic!

Since the age of five, Lesley had been having piano lessons. She took to the piano like a duck to water and would practise for hours, sitting happily alone in the big piano room. Her lessons were always on a Saturday, as school took up the week. The piano teacher, Mrs. Cowan, lived opposite in North Street, but the River Calder separated the two houses. Each Saturday Lesley would gather up her music and make her way to the piano teacher's house. Mrs. Cowan was a buxom lady with a big smile and a gentle attitude. She encouraged Lesley to play and to practise as much as she could, so that she could achieve the best grades possible in her examinations. She thought that Lesley was very talented and encouraged her to practise hard and learn to play from memory. Lesley rather fancied herself as a concert pianist; it was an ambition that would be torn away from her, just like everything else.

One day, Lesley got into a fight with a girl at school. The girl was in the next year up and quite a bit bigger than Lesley. Although Lesley was small and light on her feet, she was no match for the bigger girl, who swatted her aside like a fly. Lesley flew forward, hitting the ground hard. She picked herself and her bag up off the floor. Her knees were badly grazed and the palms of her hands were red and grazed where she had tried to stop herself falling on her face. Lesley limped home, feeling thoroughly miserable and wondering what would happen if Pam found out she had been fighting. She decided that it was probably best to say nothing and hope that nobody told on her either.

She went into the house and raced upstairs to change into her play clothes, wincing with the pain of the grazes on her hands. Then she went downstairs as she did every night, to practise the piano for an hour before dinner.

Suddenly the door burst open and there was Pam. 'I hear you had an accident today,' she said as if announcing some great event. Lesley was crestfallen; she was really rather hoping that nobody would say anything and she could pretend nothing had happened. She explained very carefully about the fight and how the girl had pushed her over.

'Yes, I already knew all that!' Pam shouted. 'Simon told me all about it.'

Lesley was furious. She had told Simon what had

happened, hoping that he might show some compassion. Instead of that, he had told Pam and now she was in trouble, again. Lesley decided that she really hated Simon too; he was a creep.

'How do you think it makes me look, a child of mine fighting in the street like some urchin from the rough area?' Pam spat the words at her.

Lesley just sat there, she knew that arguing never helped; she would only get a beating. She kept her hands poised over the next notes she was going to play on the piano. 'I think this might teach you what happens to children that fight!' Pam shouted. With that, she slammed the piano lid down onto Lesley's fingers. Lesley shrieked and sobbed as she rocked back and forth, trying to ease the double pain of the grazes on her hands and the impact of the solid wood lid on her tiny fingers. She hated this woman, she hated this house and she hated her grand-parents for making her come and live here.

Lesley ran away again in the autumn. This time she managed to walk all the way to the other side of Wishaw. A nice lady took her in and Lesley explained that she was being beaten and mistreated. The lady gave her a meal and a bed for the night. Lesley was hopeful that she had been rescued this time but her hopes were soon dashed. When she went down for breakfast the next morning, there was a policeman sitting at the table. He asked Lesley about the beatings and said that he thought she must be making this up. He had spoken to Pam and Nuri and he thought they were a very nice respectable couple, who were worried sick about her whereabouts. Lesley was furious. Would nobody ever believe her? They might well be respectable hard-working people with children of their own, but they were monsters. Lesley vowed that one day, she would expose them as the frauds they were. The policeman returned her to the house of hell, with the riding crop waiting patiently as she was brought into the house. These people are monsters, Lesley thought as she was given yet another beating.

Chapter 8

The Worst Christmas Ever

———•◦◉◦•———

Autumn passed and Christmas drew ever closer. Lesley hated Christmas. These weird people belonged to this weird Baha'i religion that didn't believe in Christmas. They still celebrated it though, after a fashion. Lesley knew that Christmas for her meant another lot of educationalss books and games, maybe some vile-coloured clothes two sizes too big, no dolls or nice-smelling talc or sweets. The highlight of Christmas for Lesley was the Honeywell Christmas party, which was always held in the Trocadero Ballroom in Hamilton. It was a fun afternoon, with games and dancing and lovely food. Santa always came down the chimney, or so it seemed to these little people. He brought each one a present – a doll or a tea set for the girls, whilst the boys had an Action Man doll or a football game. Lesley was so excited when she got her present that she ripped the paper off and opened the box to see what was inside. Each Christmas she would get home from the party and the present would be confiscated till Christmas Day.

Lesley got used to disappointment at a very young age. She knew her school friends would laugh when she told them all the boring things she had been bought. However, this Christmas was going to be a very miserable one for one unsuspecting little girl. It had been a long, cold winter. Pam and Nuri were always in a bad mood. Lesley couldn't work out whether she hated them more than they hated her. They argued constantly, and Lesley grew tired of the doors slamming and the shouting. However, the beatings lessened while they argued between themselves.

Christmas drew ever closer and Lesley was enthralled by all the decorations in the shops up Merry Street in Motherwell and the pretty fairy lights everywhere. There were no Christmas decorations in Pam and Nuri's house; they didn't believe in Christmas, so the house remained cold and unfriendly the whole year round. Lesley wished she had been adopted by a couple who actually wanted a child to love, not a live-in slave and punch bag to vent their anger on.

Every time they went out, Lesley would look wistfully at the pretty toys in the shops. There were beautiful dolls, like the new Sindy doll with a beautiful dress. Lesley so wished she could have one, but she knew better than to ever ask for anything. Lesley only had one doll, her grandma had taken pity and sent it to her, old Yvonne, the doll she had grown up with. Yvonne was now battered and dirty and Lesley wished with all her heart that she could have a new one. In previous years, one of the neighbours had given her some cowboys and Indians, what a stupid toy to give a girl. Lesley hated them and used to throw them at the wall in her frustration and anger, without Pam ever knowing, of course. She had lots of Lego, but there was a limit to the number of houses she wanted to build with it. Lesley used to build pretty houses, with trees outside. She imagined that one day she would live in a house that looked like the Lego house. Just for once, this forlorn little girl would have welcomed a really special, carefully thought out present. *One day*, she thought, *someone will buy me a present so special it will melt my heart*. Little did Lesley know that she would have to wait till she was twenty-four for that special present.

Christmas was almost upon her. The end of the school term arrived and Lesley was put to work as usual, cleaning every room. She scrubbed the skirting boards, she dusted every nook and cranny and vacuumed all the floors. Pam was now very adept at surreptitiously running her fingers along the top of the furniture or skirting board to check whether it had been properly cleaned. Since the age of six, Lesley had been told that if she did a good job she would be paid pocket money. Sadly, the money never seemed to arrive, as Pam always managed to find the one speck of dust Lesley had missed, using this as an excuse not to pay her any pocket money. Lesley had given up; she didn't actually need anything and she certainly wasn't going to ask for the money.

One week before Christmas, it happened. How it happened will remain a mystery to Lesley for the rest of her life, but she always suspected foul play in the shape of Pam or Simon.

Nuri came home from work as usual that night. He went through his usual routine. The flask and sandwich box were placed on the side in the kitchen, ready to be washed and the contents prepared for the next day. Dinner was served as usual and Lesley was left to clear the table and put everything away, while Simon did his homework and Lucy and John were put to bed by Pam.

Lesley completed all the jobs, as she did every night. She cleaned everyone's shoes, including her own, ready for the next day. Then she retreated to her bedroom to read and play till bedtime.

All of a sudden the door burst open and there stood Pam. 'You clumsy bitch!' she shouted. 'How the hell did you manage to smash Nuri's flask? You know he needs it for work tomorrow.' Lesley was puzzled. Yes, she had washed the flask, just like she had done every night for months. But it was intact when she had placed it back on the worktop, ready for Pam to fill with coffee the next morning.

Lesley was not about to admit to something she hadn't done. She looked up at Pam and said, 'I didn't break the flask. It was fine when I left it. I washed it like I do every night, the way you showed me.'

Pam insisted that the flask had been broken, so Lesley followed her to the kitchen to have a look. Pam picked up the flask and gave it to Lesley. Sure enough, all the glass interior of the flask was in a thousand pieces. Lesley was completely confused. How could this have happened? She looked up at Pam.

'Well?' Pam was clearly convinced Lesley had broken the flask, but Lesley was sure she had not broken it. After all, why would she break it, which would mean another beating?

'I swear it wasn't broken when I left it on the side,' Lesley said.

Pam was in no mood to accept this honest answer. 'Don't lie to me, bitch!' she shouted. 'Just admit you did it.' Lesley knew she wasn't going to win this time, but she was not going to admit to something she knew she hadn't done. Sensing that the girl wasn't going to back down, Pam screamed at her: 'Get out of my sight!' Lesley waited for the repercussions and beating, but they didn't happen. She knew better than to think she had heard the last of the event. Sure enough, Pam's revenge was not far away.

Christmas morning arrived and Lesley looked out of her bedroom window. She had to scrape a little of the ice from the inside of the window so that she could see the snow glistening on the neighbour's roof in the bright sunshine, the sun's rays dancing like diamonds on the snow. The grass was a beautiful white carpet, with little blades of grass that had poked their heads through to get some warmth in the sunshine. Lesley looked at the end of her bed: no present. She thought that seemed odd, so she checked outside the bedroom door: nothing there either. She thought that maybe this year, just for once, Pam and Nuri had bought her a very special present and it was downstairs. Lesley got herself washed and dressed, made her bed and went downstairs. She looked in the lounge: there were presents for everyone else, but not for her. She looked in the piano room: nothing there. Lesley was baffled, what was going on? Pam called her into the kitchen. By her side was a big sack, stuffed full of presents in beautiful glittery paper. There were little things and some in bigger boxes. Lesley's eyes lit up. 'Are those presents for me?' she asked excitedly.

Pam was smirking at her, Lesley had a bad feeling about what was about to happen. 'Do you remember how Nuri's flask got broken?' Pam asked her.

'I do, but as I said, it wasn't me.' Lesley replied.

Pam's tone hardened. 'If you admit you smashed the flask, you can have your presents.'

Lesley knew that if she admitted fault she still wouldn't get the presents, just another beating. She also knew that it was wrong to tell lies, so she stood her ground. 'You always tell me I must tell the truth,' she said. 'The truth is I did not break the flask and I would be telling lies if I said I did.'

Pam picked up the bag of presents. 'If you insist on lying about this, then you must forfeit your Christmas presents this year.' With that, she stormed out of the kitchen.

Lesley started to cry. She had never had to experience

a Christmas with no presents. She imagined how all her schoolfriends would tease and taunt her when she said she had not been given her gifts. Lesley fell to her knees and sobbed. She banged her head on the cold kitchen floor as she cried, as if to try and rid herself of the pain in her little heart. She hated this house and everything about it. She hated these monsters that had offered her a home yet now abused her every day of her life. She hated their children, who were always getting her into trouble and laughing at her when she was beaten. Lesley would not forget this Christmas ever! She vowed that one day she would escape from this place. She wondered what her sister was doing on this Christmas Day. Was she being treated the same way? Lesley really hoped not. Surely they couldn't both have been taken in by sick, sadistic people.

Christmas Day was very miserable for the little girl. She watched television while she was allowed but couldn't bring herself to laugh at the comedy shows or sing along with *Top of the Pops*. Lesley now felt totally desolate, completely abandoned by those she thought loved her. She was totally alone in this cold, violent house. She couldn't wait for school to start again.

In class, all her friends were excited, full of stories about the lovely presents they had been given for Christmas.

Her friends asked what Lesley had received for Christmas.

'Nothing,' she replied sullenly.

'What do you mean, nothing?' they asked. These children were from normal families, full of love and laughter. Some of their parents were not well-off, but they made sure their children had the best of what they could afford and they loved their children. Lesley's friends had no understanding of what it was like to live in this house of fear and violence. They thought Lesley was just making it up, even though she was covered in bruises most of the time. Lesley started to cry; she felt completely miserable.

One of her friends took her to one side. 'Is it true that you didn't get anything for Christmas?' she asked.

In between sobs, Lesley managed a 'yes'.

'That's awful,' the little girl said.

The next day, her friend came into school and ran up to Lesley in the playground. 'I've brought you a present,' she said. 'I told my mum what happened to you and she said no child should ever be without a Christmas present. This is for you.'

Lesley's little eyes lit up. 'Thank you, thank you,' she said. Lesley slowly took the pretty paper off the package, savouring the moment before the gift was revealed. Inside was the prettiest purse Lesley had ever seen. It was pink and covered in multi-coloured beads. Inside the purse was a threepenny bit. 'Oh my, I don't know what to say. It's gorgeous,' Lesley said. 'Please tell your mum she is wonderful and thank her for me.'

'I will, but tuck it away so your horrible mum can't take it away from you,' Lesley's friend said.

'Don't worry, I will,' Lesley replied as she buried her precious gift in the bottom of her school satchel.

Lesley walked home from school, feeling very happy that a complete stranger had taken pity on her. The problem was, Pam searched her school satchel every night. Lesley was never quite sure what she thought she would find in there, but she was sorely tempted to put a slimy worm or a sharp pin in the bag, just to see Pam's face. However, the prospect of yet another beating put her off that idea. Lesley knew that if Pam did find the purse, she would think Lesley had stolen it. A beating would follow and the purse would be thrown in the dustbin.

Lesley ran away again in the spring. She desperately needed someone to believe her and all she wanted was to be taken back to her grandparents in Reading, where she knew she would be loved and kept safe. Eventually, like every time before, she was found by the police. Once again, Lesley explained that she was being beaten at home and she wanted to go back to Reading, but, as usual, the police didn't believe her story, which seemed so improbable it couldn't possibly be true. Once more she was returned to Pam and Nuri. This time things were different. When she arrived back at the house with the policeman, a Baha'i friend of Nuri's had come to visit. Pam and Nuri ushered Lesley into the lounge, which she found strange. Then they left her there with the stranger. The man explained that it went against the teachings of the religion that she should run away and tell lies about Pam and Nuri. After all, they had given her a loving home and all the things her mother could never have afforded for her. She must show respect and be grateful that she was not living in total poverty. Lesley was horrified. He was actually telling her that he did not believe her version of events. Lesley vowed she would never join this crazy religion, if it condoned such abuse and violence.

As soon as the visitor left, the usual beating was dished out. Lesley, although still a small child, was getting used to the cruelty, and the hatred she felt in her heart for these people was making her stronger. *One day*, she thought to herself, *I will escape from this hell on earth and you will pay for what you are doing to me*. These evil creatures did not qualify as human beings in Lesley's eyes. They were just monsters.

The long summer holidays were approaching once

more. Lesley hated the holidays; she much preferred being at school, where she was treated well and not beaten. Every school holiday would bring a long list of jobs to be done. Weeding, washing the car, washing Harry's car when he came to visit. Cleaning out the outside dog cupboard, where the dogs had urinated and defecated whilst waiting for a walk that wasn't coming. Picking the endless fruit from the bushes at the end of the front garden. Amusing Lucy and John, which was all very well till one of them fell over and started screaming, then Lesley would be shouted at for not looking after them properly. Lesley's friends were all out in the street and down in the glen, playing and messing around. Lesley didn't dare even ask if she could join them. She resented being imprisoned with these younger brats who knew exactly how to get her into trouble with their mother.

One day, just before the last day of school, Lesley went up to bed and waited for the usual nightly visit from Pam. These visits were never to say 'goodnight' or 'sleep well'. They were usually to inspect her homework, checking that it had been completed and checking whether it was all correct. If it was found to be incorrect, the pages would be torn out of her exercise book with instructions to redo the relevant pages, no matter how long it took to do it all over again. This could happen two or three times in one night, if the homework was not of a standard that Pam thought satisfactory. Sometimes Pam would open and close all Lesley's drawers and the wardrobe. If anything displeased her, Pam would empty every drawer and every item out of the wardrobe onto the floor. Lesley would then be wrenched out of bed by her arms and forced to put the whole lot away. The next night an inspection would be done and if found to be unsatisfactory the whole lot would be tipped out once more. Lesley used to dread hearing Pam's footsteps on the staircase. She used to be even more afraid if the footsteps stopped outside her bedroom door.

Occasionally, if feeling more vicious than usual, Pam would drag Lesley out of the bed, stripping the bed down to the mattress and then making Lesley remake the bed. How Lesley despised this horrid woman. Lesley used to lie in bed and imagine ways that she could kill Pam and Nuri. She used to imagine beating them around the head with a hammer from the garage, or opening the pit in the garage floor so that they would fall in. She used to imagine setting fire to their bed while they were asleep, but then she figured that Lucy and John might die too, and they didn't deserve that.

School finished for summer and Lesley's heart sank, just as it did every holiday time. One morning just after the end of the first week, Lesley went downstairs to the kitchen. She had heard lowered voices the night before, whispering in the hallway, but she hadn't seen anyone, so she assumed it must have been Simon and a friend, or Pam whispering to Nuri. Today was different. Lesley opened the kitchen door and there, sat at the kitchen table, were her darling grandma and granddad. Lesley could barely contain the joy she felt. At last! They had come to rescue her from hell! She rushed over to them, crying with joy. Suddenly Pam shouted at Lesley to stop behaving in such a ridiculous manner and to go to her room. Lesley's heart sank; was she about to get another beating for being happy to see her grandparents? No, this time Pam gave her a big suitcase and said, 'We have decided that you might benefit from spending some time with your grandparents. Pack some of your clothes and a couple of books.'

Lesley was completely taken aback. They were actually

allowing her to leave the house? Lesley thought carefully before she opened her mouth. She didn't want to incur Pam's wrath and make her change her mind about this. 'Erm, how long will I be going for, please?' she asked, just a little bit afraid of what might come next.

'You will return the week before school goes back,' Pam replied.

Lesley could not believe her luck. She was going on holiday for eight weeks! Eight whole weeks with her dear grandparents, whom she adored more than life itself. Lesley couldn't remember the last time she had felt so happy.

'Thank you so much,' she said to Pam.

Pam looked at her, a look of cold hate in her eyes, and said, 'Don't you get telling them those stupid stories about us beating you and stuff, understand? Otherwise you will never see them again. Do I make myself perfectly clear?'

'Yes,' Lesley replied meekly. In her head she vowed that Grandma and Granddad would be told every last detail of what was going on in her sad little life. Then they would feel sorry for her and she hoped that she wouldn't have to come back to Motherwell, ever.

Lesley packed her things, she packed as much as she could get in the suitcase, she was determined that she would do her utmost not to have to come back to this horrible house and these horrible people who made her so miserable.

As she finished, Pam appeared in the doorway of her bedroom. 'All done?'

'Yes, I'm finished now,' Lesley said. She thought for one awful moment that Pam had changed her mind and she wasn't going to get to go on this holiday, but this time was different. 'I'm sure your grandparents would love to buy you some new clothes, so please get a new cardigan, some new underwear and new shoes.'

Lesley nodded. She hoped that she wasn't coming back, so for now she wasn't going to worry.

Lesley raced downstairs to tell her granddad he could fetch her suitcase from her bedroom. Rustom came up the stairs. Lesley thought he was moving a bit slower than she remembered, then she realised she hadn't seen him for years and he was growing older.

He picked up the suitcase. 'Goodness me! What have you got in here?' Granddad chuckled as he struggled to lift it. Lesley laughed as she followed him down the stairs. 'Right then,' Granddad said. 'Here's the taxi, we're off now.'

Pam came to the door and as Lesley walked away, she grabbed her arm in a vice-like grip. 'Remember, if you misbehave, you'll be in big trouble when you get back.' Lesley pulled away from her. She wasn't coming back here, ever. How wrong she was.

Banoo and Rustom put their case and Lesley's onto the overnight coach. Lesley clambered aboard eagerly. Last time she had done this trip, she had been ripped away from the two people who really cared about her. That was never going to happen again. Lesley tapped her granddad on the shoulder. 'How long does it take to get to Reading?' she asked. Rustom looked puzzled. 'Reading? My darling girl, we haven't lived in Reading for years! We live in Hove now. It's a lovely place by the seaside.' Lesley thought she had died and gone to heaven. She was with her lovely grandparents and they lived by the sea. What more could she ask for? Lesley pictured her new life in this place called Hove. She had no idea where it could be, apart from somewhere on the coast.

Lesley turned to Banoo, whose hair was now completely white. 'Grandma, why don't you live in Reading any more?'

Her grandmother put her arm round the little girl. Lesley flinched as she reached out to her, which Banoo found strange. Perhaps she just needed time to get used to them being around her again, she thought to herself. She couldn't help but notice how sad she looked. Lesley's beautiful long hair was gone and she had a terribly boyish hairstyle, which didn't suit her thin frame at all. Banoo felt sad. She had never wanted the little girl to go, but she and Rustom just could not cope with a young child at their age. 'Well darling, Reading is getting very big and busy. Granddad and I struggle to get around so we thought somewhere quieter by the sea would be nice.' The coach rumbled on into the night and Lesley fell asleep leaning against her grandmother, dreaming of a new life by the coast. If only she knew that this would remain a dream.

Chapter 9

The Perfect Holiday

◦◦◦

Lesley woke from her slumbers just as the sun was coming up. The coach had just pulled into Victoria coach station. Banoo and Rustom took Lesley to the café for a cup of tea and some toast. Lesley realised that the journey wasn't over yet; they had to catch a second coach to get them to Hove. Lesley didn't mind. She was safe with her grandparents and happier than she had been for years.

They all sat in the café and watched as coaches came and went, going to and coming from destinations all over the country. Lesley was so excited she could only manage half a cup of tea and a tiny piece of toast. Instead of yelling at her and slapping her like Pam would have done, Banoo gave her a great big hug and chuckled. 'Calm down, darling. You'll make yourself sick!' Lesley tried to sit still, but she was just too excited. Rustom polished off the rest of Lesley's toast and at last they were ready to board the next coach, bound for Brighton. The coach was green this time and much more comfy than the one from Scotland. Lesley gazed out at the fields full of cows and sheep. The sun was shining and there wasn't a cloud in the sky. The scenery looked delightful, but Lesley wanted to see the sea.

Around midday they arrived at the bus station in Brighton. As the coach turned off the main road, Lesley spotted the sea and tapped Banoo on the shoulder. 'I can see the sea!' she announced. All the passengers clambered off the coach and gathered their suitcases from the luggage compartment underneath. Banoo and Rustom ushered Lesley to the taxi rank, where once more the cases were loaded in to the boot of a car. The taxi drove along the seafront towards Hove. Lesley thought how pretty it looked as the sunshine glinted on the waves, which twinkled as if sprinkled with fairy dust. There were people jogging, walking dogs; there were fancy motorbikes parked up; it all looked so wonderful. The taxi finally arrived at Ventnor Villas in Hove. The street was lined with big, old trees which formed a canopy over their heads, sheltering them from the midday sun. The converted Victorian mansion, which was now three flats, looked lovely from the outside. It had big bay windows at the front and lovely white pillars either side of the front door. Banoo and Rustom explained that they lived in the middle flat, which was on the first floor. They told Lesley that she mustn't make a noise, as the Elliotts who lived underneath were very grumpy and complained at every little noise. Lesley surveyed the scene for a moment then turned to Banoo. 'I love it here, Grandma,' she said. Lesley slowly turned round then started jumping up and down and dancing round in circles. 'I can see the sea, I can see the sea!' she chanted excitedly. Banoo and Rustom looked at each other. This little girl was going to need a lot of love and tenderness to calm the hysteria in her voice.

'Come along now,' Banoo said firmly.

Lesley followed her grandparents up the stone steps, and then Rustom unlocked the big white front door. They stepped inside and Lesley saw the door on the left. *That must belong to the Elliotts*, she thought to herself. Rustom started to climb the stairs, which led to a tiny landing and two doors. There was another staircase, which led to the top flat. Rustom unlocked the door to their flat, the one on the left above the grumpy Elliotts. He pushed the door open and ushered Lesley and Banoo inside.

Lesley looked around. She was immediately struck by how light it was. No dark, dismal passageways like the house in Motherwell. Everywhere was brightly decorated, with pretty carpet and lovely pictures on the wall. It smelt fresh and clean, not stifling and smelly like the house in Motherwell. Lesley had never seen any modern furniture. Everything in Pam and Nuri's house was supposed to be modern, but it looked like something out of the ark!

'Would you like to see your bedroom?' Banoo asked. Lesley nodded. She knew that this bedroom wouldn't be anything like the cold, uninviting bedroom she had been allocated in the cold, uninviting house she was forced to call home. Banoo opened the door and Rustom carried her suitcase in and placed it on the floor.

'Well? What do you think then? We had it specially decorated for you.' Rustom said.

Lesley looked at the pretty carpet which was cream with pink flowers on it. Cream carpet! Flowers! Her bedroom in Motherwell was like a prison cell – dull, with dowdy wallpaper and dull bedding. Lesley allowed her eyes to survey the rest of the room. There was a single bed, with the prettiest pink bedspread she had ever seen. On the pillow was a big teddy bear. 'Whose teddy is that?' Lesley asked.

'It's yours darling, you can take it home with you after your holiday and keep it in your bedroom.' Lesley's little face screwed up into a scowl. 'What is that look for?' Banoo asked. She was puzzled by the little girl's reaction. Most little girls loved teddy bears. 'But Grandma, if I take Teddy back to Motherwell, Pam will take him away and throw him in the bin. That's what she does with nice things that people buy me.'

Banoo half-suspected that this might be the case. She had never taken to this arrogant English woman and her husband. They oozed affluence, but under the surface Banoo felt uncomfortable. She had not been happy with the idea that the two sisters should be separated and adopted individually. Banoo had wanted them to be kept together. However, as a wife did in those days, she did as she was told and allowed Rustom to make the final decision. Rustom wasn't particularly happy either, but Pam and Nuri were the only two who had come forward and offered to take Lesley. Banoo sat down on the bed and picked up the teddy bear. 'Come and sit here with me, darling,' she said. Lesley happily sat down beside her and rested her head on Banoo's shoulder. 'Now, you listen to me,' Banoo said. 'This teddy is yours and nobody is going to take it away, throw it away or anything else.'

Lesley really wanted to believe her grandmother but she knew only too well what was going to happen to the beautiful soft teddy they had bought for her. That vile cruel Pam would soon throw it away, in an effort to remind Lesley that she did not deserve such nice things. Lesley had some questions she needed to ask Banoo and Rustom, but for now she was content to enjoy the flat and tell them all about her school, her lovely friends and the nice teachers. Lesley didn't know if Banoo and Rustom knew about her running away nearly every year, so she thought she would keep that quiet, unless they mentioned it. Lesley got herself ready for bed that night, feeling safer and happier than she had felt since her days in Reading. A very tired but happy little girl climbed into bed that night, dreaming of a trip to the beach the next day.

After Lesley had gone to bed and Banoo and Rustom were sure she had fallen asleep, they sat down together over a cup of cocoa and tried to work out why their granddaughter seemed so afraid of everyone. Lesley was quiet and withdrawn when other people were around, as if she was afraid to speak. If anyone reached out towards her, she would duck out of the way or flinch, as if expecting a punch or a slap. Banoo and Rustom were troubled by this. They made up their minds to have a chat with the little girl before she went home. Rustom and Banoo both wished that age had not been against them when Raymond died. The two sisters would have been much better off with their own flesh and blood. They both also hoped that the two sisters would never find out what really happened to their father. They went to bed that night totally exhausted.

The next morning, Lesley woke up to the sound of the birds singing in the trees and the sun streaming into her bedroom. She yawned and sat up in bed. She could hear Banoo clattering around in the kitchen and singing to herself. Lesley was not used to feeling happy and safe but she was going to savour every minute while it lasted. She washed and dressed and went through to the kitchen to join her grandparents. Banoo gave her a cup of tea and, after much deliberation, Lesley decided she would like a boiled egg and soldiers for breakfast. The egg arrived with lovely crispy toast soldiers, done to perfection. When Pam cooked boiled eggs, the albumen was all runny; in fact, the egg was almost raw! Lesley demolished her breakfast and helped her grandmother wash and dry the dishes.

'Now then,' Banoo said. 'I need some shopping this morning. We are going to take you to George Street, then we'll show you Blatchington Road, where there are some more shops.'

Lesley was very excited. She was not often allowed to go to town on her own in Motherwell. The furthest she ever

106

got was the grocer up the road. Pam would make her a list and give her some money. When the items were bought, Lesley had to return straight home, where she was asked to account for every penny and make sure the change was correct. 'You need to learn to count money,' Pam would say every time.

There was no such drudgery here. The shops in George Street were many and varied. Butcher, baker, grocer, fishmonger ... Lesley thought it was all so exciting. Banoo and Rustom bought her crisps, cakes and sweets, things she was never allowed in Pam's house, unless guests were expected. Over the next few weeks, Lesley was taken out daily by her grandparents. She visited Shoreham, Worthing, Brighton, Lewes and Newhaven. Lesley liked Brighton. It was a busy town with lots of shops and thousands of people. Rustom explained that a lot of them were on holiday, just like Lesley. There was nobody telling her off, no slaps, no beatings. Lesley was having a ball.

It was during this holiday that Lesley met her uncle. He came to visit Banoo and Rustom. His name was Roy and he lived in Brighton with his wife Dorothy. Banoo and Rustom explained that Roy was Lesley's mum's brother. The whole family had relocated from Reading to Brighton and Hove in dribs and drabs. Uncle Roy was funny, affectionate and a bit eccentric. Lesley thought she liked him, but she wasn't sure. If he was her mum's brother, where was her real mother?

One day, Uncle Roy offered to take Lesley out for the afternoon. His house was two bus rides away, so Lesley thought this would be a great adventure. The old bus creaked and groaned as it followed the bus route through the streets until Uncle Roy said it was time to get off. Lesley held his hand as she tried to negotiate the high step from the bus onto the kerb. 'How much further is your house?' she asked.

'Not far now,' he said. They walked along a bit before turning up a narrow side street. Uncle Roy opened the door to a tiny little terraced house and Lesley followed him inside.

'Where is Auntie Dorothy?' she asked him.'

'She's at work,' he replied.

Lesley was a little uncomfortable with this reply. 'So why have you brought me here?' she asked him.

Roy was careful in his choice of words. He had thoughts in mind that this little girl would not have been happy about. She was far too naïve and scared to ever tell on him. 'I thought you might like a break away from my mum and dad. You know how Granddad carries on about everything.' Lesley smiled, she knew what he meant. Granddad's intentions were genuine. He wanted Lesley to do well at school, to study hard and perhaps go to university. But she was only nine years old, almost ten! Uncle Roy offered Lesley a drink and a biscuit. Then he said, 'Would you like me to take your photo? You have a very pretty face.'

Nobody had ever told Lesley she was pretty. Pam and Nuri had told her plenty of times that she was stupid, ugly, a slut (whatever that was), a bitch, but pretty? Lesley's little heart lifted when she heard that word.

'Yes please, Uncle. That would be nice, then Grandma and Granddad can have a photo of me to keep.'

Uncle Roy looked at Lesley. He thought how innocent she looked, how easy it would be for him to coax her to do his bidding. That would come later.

Roy was a photographer by trade. Lesley thought his collection of cameras and lenses was a little excessive, but if she had known the truth about why there were so many (which years later she did), she would have realised what they were all used for. Roy took some photos of Lesley and promised to get them printed. The other photos in his dirty little mind could be done another day.

Roy decided it was time to take his niece back to her grandparents. He didn't want to frighten her with his devious ideas on her first visit here. *Build her confidence slowly*, he thought, *then she'll do anything I say.* He gathered up their jackets and they headed back to Hove, on the same bus with the squealing brakes.

Lesley settled easily into her grandparents' daily routine. Breakfast was followed by a short walk to George Street or Blatchington Road to buy food such as tasty fresh bread and cream cakes. Sometimes Banoo and Rustom would take Lesley on the bus to Brighton, where they would buy her an ice cream on the seafront.

Lesley remembered that she was to ask for a new cardigan and some new underwear, as well as new shoes. She broached the subject on one of the many outings to Brighton. Banoo and Rustom were more than happy to oblige. They took Lesley into the big Marks & Spencer store. Lesley had never been in such a lovely shop. It had a distinct lovely smell and all the clothes were bright and inviting.

Banoo took Lesley to where the cardigans were. 'Now then, darling, which colour would you like?' Lesley thought long and hard. Pam hadn't specified a colour; she just said that Lesley was to ask for a new cardigan.

Lesley chose her cardigan. It was a beautiful apricot colour, and it jumped out at her as she inspected all the colours on the shelf. Lesley took it down. 'Try it on,' Banoo said. Lesley slipped the cardigan on. It didn't feel like the rough wool Pam knitted with. This cardigan was silky soft and as Lesley put it on, she could feel the warmth of the wool against her skin. 'Oh, darling, that looks so pretty on you, don't you think so, Rustom?'

Rustom smiled at his granddaughter. She looked so pretty in her new cardigan. Rustom couldn't imagine that such treats were very frequent in Pam's household. 'Oh yes, that looks lovely. Give it to me. I will go and pay the lady,' Rustom said. Once the cardigan was paid for, Lesley asked if she could carry the bag. She had never had such a pretty item of clothing, leave alone one that fitted her properly.

Next was the underwear. Banoo and Rustom decided that Littlewoods was a good shop, so they took Lesley in to see if they could find her something. Lesley found a pretty vest and pants set, with little lace panels and flowers on. Banoo bought two of these sets in different colours. After all, the child would need to change her underwear! As Lesley had not developed a bust, there was no need for a bra at this point. Lesley now had two carrier bags with her new clothes in. She was positively bursting with pride and couldn't wait to tell Pam how Grandma and Granddad had taken her to Marks & Spencer and Littlewoods.

Lesley forgot her fear just for a moment. She would remember it all too soon.

The next day, Uncle Roy came round again. He took Lesley out to Brighton and bought her a burger and some chips in the Wimpy bar down West Street. Lesley had never had a burger before; this was a whole new experience and she enjoyed the new taste.

Next, Uncle Roy suggested that perhaps he could buy Lesley some new shoes. Lesley loved the shoe shops along Western Road. There were so many to choose from.

True-Form, Barratts, Stead and Simpson, Bata, Russell & Bromley. Lesley made Uncle Roy walk all the way along the street, looking into every shop window. Suddenly Lesley saw her dream shoes on a rack outside True-Form. They were red sandals, with just the hint of a grown-up heel. Lesley fell in love with them. 'Please, Uncle! Please can I have those red ones? They're so pretty!' Lesley was beside herself with excitement.

Uncle Roy was not too sure. He and his wife Dorothy had not been blessed with children and he had no idea what would be considered suitable footwear for a nine-year-old. 'I think we had better ask Grandma first, don't you?' Uncle said.

But Lesley was having none of it. Those sandals had her name on them! 'But if we don't get them now, they'll be gone and I won't get any,' she wailed.

Uncle Roy thought that she was probably right, so he took her into the shop to have her feet measured.

The sales lady was very nice and sat them down. 'Now then, young lady, what size shoe do you take?' she asked Lesley.

'I'm a size eleven, miss,' Lesley said in her best grown-up voice. The lady went off to fetch the gadget that would confirm Lesley's shoe size. 'I'm sorry to tell you, you are not size eleven. You are a size one,' the lady said.

'But I can't be,' Lesley replied. 'These shoes and my school shoes are an eleven.'

The sales lady looked at Uncle Roy. 'Who is this child's parent?' she demanded sternly.

'Not me,' Uncle Roy replied.

'Well, you tell her parents that she is wearing shoes that are three sizes too small! Disgraceful!' the lady said.

After much tutting and reiteration by the sales lady,

Lesley emerged with her lovely red sandals. If she'd had a chest to puff out, it would have been more than obvious to everyone just how proud she was of her new sandals. However, fear lurked in the back of her mind as she tried to imagine what Pam would say when she headed back at the end of the holidays. For now, she would wear her sandals every day, all day! This would prove to be a very wise decision. Uncle Roy suggested to Lesley that they should go to his house for a couple of hours, as Auntie Dorothy would be there this time. Lesley agreed, feeling happier that this time she would meet his wife for the first time.

It was not a happy event. Auntie Dorothy had a very nervous disposition and did not like any noise in the house. Lesley found out that she worked as a typist in the civil service. Auntie Dorothy was not at all welcoming and Lesley felt that she was not wanted in the home. She sat and drank her squash quietly, not daring to speak. Eventually Auntie Dorothy announced that she was going for a lie-down. Lesley thought that her uncle might decide to return her to her grandparent's home, but he had other ideas. He suggested to Lesley that she might like to pose for him like some of his models did. Lesley hadn't a clue what he was talking about; the only model she had ever seen on television was Twiggy. Her uncle showed Lesley some photos of ladies, but they had no clothes on.

Lesley was horrified! She had never seen a fully grown naked woman and was not too happy about this. 'I'm not taking my clothes off,' she announced defiantly.

Her uncle assured her that he did not expect her to do this, but instead to sit in the same position as the lady in the photo.

Lesley was happy to do that and chatted nineteen to the dozen while Uncle snapped away with the camera. He made her sit on the floor with her hand between her thighs, which Lesley found a bit odd. She couldn't imagine why anyone could think that made a nice photo for their album.

Lesley asked Uncle Roy to take some photos of her head and shoulders, so that she could give some more photos to her grandparents before she returned home. Uncle Roy took a few more frames before suggesting they should get back to his parents' home for Lesley to have her evening meal. They climbed aboard the bus back to Hove, where Banoo had been baking, and Lesley took no persuading when she was asked to sample the cakes.

Lesley was all too aware that the end of the school holidays was approaching fast. Banoo and Rustom did their best to assure her that she must go back north but that they would speak to Pam about these beatings and cruel incidents.

Lesley still felt no better. She had a horrible feeling that life was not going to be any different, whatever her grandparents might have to say to Pam. Lesley had felt totally relaxed with her grandparents, and they made her feel at home in their little flat. They didn't shout at her, they didn't beat her and they treated her like a human being, not a servant.

Lesley was determined that before she went back, she would find out what had happened to her father and where her sister was. Her opportunity came one afternoon, while she was sat with her grandparents enjoying some of Banoo's delicious cake.

Lesley took a deep breath. 'Granddad, can I ask you a question, please?'

'Of course you can darling, what is it?' Rustom was curious to know what the question was going to be.

Lesley carried on. 'What happened to my daddy? Don't

tell me he died of a bad tummy, because my friends at school said nobody dies of a bad tummy.'

Rustom was taken aback, this was not the question he had expected from such a young child. Rustom thought that Lesley was so young when she was taken to Scotland that he was surprised that she even remembered what had happened all those years ago. Little did he know that this little girl had thought of little else for many years. 'You have a good memory,' Rustom said. 'We thought that you and Karen were too young to understand and, to be perfectly honest, the truth was so awful, we weren't sure how to tell you.' Rustom carried on. This next sentence was going to be a bombshell for this little girl. With a deep breath and a very heavy heart, Rustom said, 'Your daddy committed suicide, darling. Do you know what that means?'

Lesley did know, but she didn't want to think that her daddy had been so unhappy that he didn't want to live any more. 'How did Daddy, you know, do it?' Lesley asked, not sure if she even wanted to know the answer.

'Your daddy gassed himself, sweetheart. He put his head in the oven and turned the gas on. Because the gas is poisonous, it killed him.' Lesley thought this sounded a horrible way to die – slow and painful. She also figured that if the gas was poisonous, she was never going to have a gas cooker in her house. Lesley thought for a moment, then the memory of her mother sat on the floor crying came flooding back and she shuddered.

Rustom took Lesley's tiny trembling hand. He didn't like to lie to his granddaughter; she was a bright intelligent girl and wouldn't settle for being fobbed off with lies. 'This is what happened,' Rustom continued. 'Your dad came home for lunch as usual. After lunch, he gave your mum some money and told her to take you and Karen into town to buy you some new clothes. While you were all out of the house, he gassed himself. When Mummy returned with you two, she found him on the kitchen floor. One of the neighbours took you and Karen in, till we could get there to remove you from the house. You see, the police had to investigate and find out exactly what had happened that day.'

Lesley was listening very carefully to every word being said, trying to imagine her poor lovely daddy inhaling the noxious gas fumes, knowing that he was going to die. Lesley could not understand why her dad would want to kill himself. Worse still, he had abandoned his two little girls. Lesley really wanted to know why, but if Granddad didn't know, nobody else would. A new set of questions came into her head. She needed answers, if she was going to be beaten and mistreated for the rest of her life, she needed to know why. 'Granddad, why couldn't Mummy look after me and Karen?' she asked Rustom.

He thought for what seemed to Lesley like an eternity, but he didn't quite know what to say. Lesley would be sixteen before she met her mother again and the realisation of why would be only too clear. Rustom spoke again. 'Well, darling, it's like this. Mummy was only young then. When Daddy died, she had no idea how she would manage, as your daddy was the only one working and your mum had no income. Mummy couldn't afford to feed or clothe you. Instead of asking for help, your mum brought you both to us to look after you properly. After that, she more or less abandoned you and left Grandma and myself to look after you. We were too old to look after you on a long-term basis, which is why you have both been adopted.'

Lesley could not believe what she was hearing. The fact

that her dad had killed himself was bad enough. To then discover that their mother had abandoned them both was just too much. Lesley was angry with her father. If he had not committed suicide, none of this would have happened. The family would still be together and the two girls would not have been separated. Lesley hated her mother for dumping her and her sister with their grandparents. She would never forgive her for that. Lesley turned to her granddad once more. 'Granddad, because of all this, I have to live with Pam and Nuri forever. If that is right, I am not happy. I really hate them!' Lesley announced.

Rustom was not surprised; he had always had a bad feeling about those two. Besides, if it was so nice there, why had Lesley kept running away from them? For now he tried to smooth things over, hoping that things might improve at some point.

'Where is my sister?' Lesley asked, before Rustom had chance to open his mouth. 'I have a sister and I want to know where she is. Why does she never come to see me?'

Rustom once more braced himself for the next showdown. 'Yes, of course you have a sister, darling. Karen has been adopted by a lovely couple on the Isle of Man. She has some sisters of her own now and is very happy.' Lesley had no idea where the Isle of Man was; she had never heard of such a place.

'Can't I write to my sister?' she asked Rustom. He wasn't sure that Karen's adopted parents would approve of opening up old wounds, but they were good Christians and looked after Karen very well. Rustom promised Lesley that he would find out if Karen would be allowed to write. He was more worried that Lesley may not be allowed access to her sister.

Rustom was finding this conversation very difficult. All

the events of years ago were now having serious repercussions. Whilst Karen was being brought up in a loving household, it was clear that Lesley had not been quite so lucky. Rustom vowed that all would eventually turn out for the best. Convincing himself of this was the hardest part.

Lesley was easily distracted when Rustom suggested he take her down to the seafront to get an ice cream. Lesley's eyes lit up straight away. She loved being by the sea. She could gaze out and dream about adventures on a boat. She also loved the little shop down on the front. It was like Aladdin's cave. There were buckets and spades, sun hats, flip flops, snorkel goggles and some very naughty postcards. The best bit was the lovely ice cream.

The end of the week grew closer and Lesley started to get jittery at the thought of having to go back to Scotland. She wished she could stay with her grandparents in this lovely place called Hove forever. Banoo and Rustom tried to distract Lesley by taking her out on the bus. They went into Brighton, where they bought her some colouring pencils and a sketchbook. They bought her a little camera and a snow globe with a picture of the Brighton Dome inside. Next they bought her some new clothes, new tops, new trousers, new pyjamas. Banoo thought that by doing this Lesley would remember them every time she put the clothes on.

The day dawned when Lesley had to return to Scotland. She was miserable and kept crying, saying she was afraid to go back. She couldn't eat, and she felt sick.

Banoo helped her pack all her lovely new things into a big holdall, along with the suitcase she had arrived with. Her grandparents took her for one last look at the sea, and then it was over. This time her grandfather took her on the long coach journey. There was no laughter now, just fear and tears as the coach sped further north. Rustom tried his hardest to cheer his granddaughter up, but to no avail. The terror in her heart threatened to engulf her. Once more, she felt alone and terrified of what awaited her in Motherwell. The coach eventually reached Glasgow, from where the connecting bus would take them to Motherwell. Lesley's heart was beating so hard she feared it might burst out of her chest. A taxi took them the last part of the journey. As it pulled up outside the house, Lesley felt very sick and her heart sank into her shoes. The terror that had gripped her when she first arrived in this hell now returned for a second time. Her legs turned to jelly and she started to tremble as she walked, very, very slowly, up the path behind her granddad. She wondered what torture was awaiting her behind the prison door. She would never call this house her home. It was cold, uninviting and had an air of fear about it, even from the outside.

Pam came to the door, all smiles and sweetness, and greeted Rustom like a long-lost friend. Lesley however, was not fooled by the false smiles. She knew only too well what would happen when her grandfather left to travel home. Pam made a pot of tea and put some biscuits on a plate on the table. Lesley was hungry, but she didn't dare take one without being offered one. Her grandparents had allowed her to take whatever food she wanted during her stay there. How different those last six weeks had been.

'I have a surprise for you,' Pam said. Lesley wondered what sort of surprise they could possibly have for her. 'As we missed your tenth birthday, we've decorated your bedroom while you've been away as a special present,' she said. 'Go and have a look.'

Lesley looked at her granddad, who was smiling at her.

He promised to come and have a look in a minute, but he wanted to speak to Pam for a moment. Lesley knew what that meant: Granddad was going to tackle Pam about the beatings she had dished out to Lesley. She was petrified. She knew that any conversation would not be met kindly and she would be the one to pay the price.

Lesley trudged up to her bedroom and opened the door. The room looked completely different. Gone was the clinical white woodchip paper that had been on the walls. Instead, there was pretty wallpaper with ladies on it, dressed in varying clothes, all different shades of pinks. There were new pretty pink curtains and a lovely fashionable nylon bedspread. The wardrobes had been painted white; Lesley could detect just the hint of a smell of white gloss paint. There was a smart new desk on which she could do her homework or read.

Lesley tried her very hardest to feel excited. She tried to force her mouth into a smile but it didn't happen. The room might have been decorated, but it was still cold like the house. There was no love in this house; it felt like an ice house and her bedroom still felt the same. All Lesley could feel was afraid and lonely.

After what seemed like an age, Rustom came up to inspect the newly decorated bedroom. Pam was close behind, no doubt making sure they didn't talk about her, Lesley thought. When she saw Pam's face, the look was not one of pleasure, but rather that look that threatened violence as soon as the opportunity arose. 'This is lovely, darling,' Rustom said. 'Aren't you lucky to have such a lovely new room and such a lovely house to live in.'

Lesley wanted to laugh out loud. If only Rustom knew what was going to happen when he left. Lesley stayed quiet. In her heart, she vowed that one day, when she escaped from here, everyone would know about the monsters that lived in this house and how they had treated her.

The day drew to a close and, just as her grandmother had done all those years ago, her grandfather had to leave to get the coach home. Lesley clung to him and begged him to take her back with him, but Pam dug her nails into Lesley's arm, telling her in her own cruel way that there was no escape from this hell. As Rustom walked down the path to his taxi, Lesley watched him leave and sobbed till she thought her heart would break. She had left this house all those weeks ago hoping never to return, but now she was back in hell, with the monsters waiting to pounce once more.

Chapter 10

Growing Up

———•☙❧•———

As soon as her granddad was gone, Lesley shut her prison door behind her. She had known, hours ago, by the look on Pam's face, that she was in serious trouble. Pam called her into the kitchen and told her to sit down. 'How was your holiday? Did you have a nice time?' she asked.

Lesley nodded lamely. She wondered where this conversation was leading.

'At what point did you decide to tell you grandparents a pack of lies?' Pam asked her.

Lesley was only little, but already her hatred for this woman and this house was giving her more inner strength on a daily basis. The more Pam shouted and kept on, the more Lesley despised her.

'Your grandfather has just told me that apparently we beat you all the time, we don't allow you to go out and play with your friends, your clothes and shoes never fit you properly so you are the object of ridicule all the time.'

Pam was angry and Lesley knew it was pointless trying to reason with this monster. She sat silently, waiting for what would happen next. Pam was in full flow now, so she carried on. 'Have you ever thought why we need to beat you, you stupid, thick bitch? If you did as you were told, you wouldn't get any beatings, would you? If you did everything asked of you, we wouldn't need to beat you. If you didn't run away, we wouldn't need to beat you.' Lesley looked at Pam with utter hatred in her eyes. If she had the courage, she would stick a knife in her throat and laugh out loud as Pam bled to death in front of her. *Another day*, she thought to herself. *Your time will come.* She soon came round to the stark reality that no matter what she did or said, there were plenty of years of hell waiting for her in this house. Pam marched Lesley upstairs to her room. *Oh no*, Lesley thought, *a beating already and I only got home six hours ago*. Pam opened the suitcase and looked at the beautiful apricot-coloured cardigan that her loving grandparents had bought for her. Lesley had worn it every day since the day it was bought, she loved the vibrant colour and the soft feel of the wool. Pam pulled it from the case.

'What the bloody hell is this?' she raged.

Lesley explained that her grandmother had bought it for her, as instructed by Pam.

'You stupid, disobedient, thick cow! I said you had to get a cardigan for school!'

Lesley thought back to the original instruction. No, Pam definitely didn't say the cardigan was for school. No good arguing; that would just encourage Pam to beat her and she hadn't missed the beatings one bit during the holidays. Pam opened Lesley's bedroom window and threw the cardigan out.

'But that's my favourite cardigan!' Lesley shouted with dismay.

'I don't care whether it is. I told you to get a cardigan for school! Since when is your school uniform orange?' Pam yelled.

Lesley wasn't about to let this go. She loved that cardigan, her grandparents had bought it for her and she wasn't going to be beaten into submission this time. 'You can't do that!' Lesley shouted at Pam. The fist caught her back, taking her breath away. Lesley started to cry. She knew this would happen.

Pam pulled out the new underwear without comment. It was put to one side. Her new skirt, also a pretty colour, joined the cardigan outside. Lesley could not understand why. It was pretty, it was a decent length, but she thought she had better keep quiet, lest another fist made contact. Lesley was dreading Pam finding the sandals. She could have predicted what would happen, but she waited. Sure enough: 'What the bloody hell are these?' Pam shouted. She was waving the sandals in the air, like an alien who had found something it had never seen before.

'Sandals,' Lesley replied cockily. She was tiring of this game.

'I can see that,' Pam said. First, one sandal hit Lesley in the face, closely followed by the second. 'Throw them out!' Pam demanded.

Lesley did as she was told. She couldn't wait to tell her grandparents what Pam had done. At that moment, Lesley wished she was dead. Better still, she wished Pam would die. She hated her; she couldn't think of anyone she hated more. That night, when Lesley went to bed, she curled up in a ball under the covers and sobbed and sobbed. How different this was from last week, when her grandma had come in every night and tucked her in, giving her a hug before she went to sleep. Lesley was very angry and bitter. Once more she took the cord from her dressing gown and tied it round her neck, pulling it ever tighter. She didn't care if she died; nobody loved her in this house and they were going to keep her prisoner forever.

Her mission was rudely interrupted by the sound of footsteps on the stairs. She quickly loosened the cord and dived back under the covers, in case Pam was on the rampage again.

*

The new school term started and Lesley went back to join her friends once more. Many of them had been away to the seaside and all compared notes about where they had been, how sunny it was and how nice the ice cream tasted. For once, Lesley was able to tell them, honestly, that she had enjoyed her summer holiday. She thought better of telling them what had happened when she returned to Motherwell. Now that Lesley was ten, Pam finally sat her down and said that from now on she would be given a rise in her pocket money for any jobs she did around the house. Lesley thought this was a great idea as it meant she would be able to buy sweets from the shop, or a comic if she fancied it. Lesley dusted, hoovered, did the washing up and drying up, she made the sandwiches for the next day for all the children, she helped hang out the washing and bring it in. Lesley thought that as she had been doing all these things for years, without ever being paid, now was as good a time as any to earn some money. That was easier said than done. Pam extended the list to whatever jobs she had no desire to complete. Pam would check every window ledge and corner before she paid Lesley.

In her final year at primary school, field trips were organised for the children. Lesley brought the form home and showed Pam. Pam said that if Lesley completed all her jobs and saved her money, she could go on the trip. Lesley tried really hard. She did all the cleaning. She helped look after the younger children. She washed the car and walked the dogs. Pam always found some excuse as to why she should not be paid for the work she had completed. Knowing how desperately Lesley wanted to go on the trip, Nuri took pity on her and gave her the money for the trip. However, although she enjoyed the day out, Lesley could not go to the shop and buy sweets like her friends as she had no money left. That would not change until Lesley went out to work.

Lesley's last year at primary school was very difficult. Hormones were starting to kick in and Lesley's periods started. Lesley had no idea what was happening to her. Nobody had explained about this event, which every woman has to deal with. Lesley didn't want a repeat of the soiled underpants event, but she was terrified that she might bleed to death if she didn't speak up. Lesley went home from school, having used most of the shiny school tissue paper to try and absorb the blood.

When Pam came home, Lesley explained what had happened. To her utter amazement, Pam was very understanding. She explained in full the facts of life to Lesley. From a drawer in her bedroom, Pam pulled out what looked like a miniature hammock and a thick wadded pad. She showed Lesley how to put the two together to form a sanitary belt, which Pam said would absorb the blood, as long as Lesley changed it often. Lesley confided in one of her friends at school about this new phenomenon in her life and how she had to wear a sanitary pad and belt. Her friend laughed and said that her mum had bought her Tampax, as they were discreet and worn internally, which was much easier. Lesley thought she would ask Pam if she could have some of the Tampax, instead of this cumbersome belt and pad, which moved and leaked and made her feel dirty, even though she wasn't.

Pam was less than understanding. She explained that any female in the Baha'i faith had to be a virgin when she married. If Lesley wore Tampax, it could inadvertently break her virginity and she would bring disgrace on the family. Lesley thought this was utter bunkum, but she had no choice but to obey. Every time she had an accident and soiled her pants with blood, she would be made to wash these by hand, rubbing salt into the stain to remove it till her hands bled. Such humiliation was never forgotten.

The next hurdle to get over was the choice of secondary school. In those days, when catchment areas were much closer to home, the town of Motherwell was divided by the main road, Merry Street. On one side was Braidhurst, the comprehensive school. On the other side was Dalziel High School, considered to be better. Lesley's school was designated as Braidhurst, which caused a great furore in the household. Pam, a teacher herself, was a snob and there was no way she was going to allow any child in her household to go to this rough (in her opinion) school, where all the children from the council estates went (her words). She insisted that Lesley should sit an eleven plus exam for Hutcheson's Girl's Grammar School in Glasgow, a private school. Lesley was horrified. She wanted to go the comprehensive or to Dalziel High with her friends. She didn't want to go to the posh private grammar school.

The day arrived and Lesley was marched to Motherwell station to get the train to Pollockshaws, and then a short walk took them to the school. Pam was adamant that Lesley should be able to pass the entrance exam without difficulty. Lesley thought that deliberately failing the exam would prove harder, but she was going to try anyway. Lesley sat the exam, trying hard to get some of the answers wrong. Some of the papers were hard and the whole process seemed to go on for hours. Eventually she had completed all the papers. The head teacher said she would inform Pam of the results within a few weeks. Lesley was praying that she had failed the exam. She didn't want to go to the posh school with the posh children. She wanted to be with the friends she had grown up with.

Eventually, the results arrived. By some fluke, Lesley had passed the entrance exam. Her heart sank. That meant a very early start in the morning, followed by a long walk to the station, then a train journey to school. To make matters worse, Lesley would have to wear a stupid uniform with a stupid hat. A hat, for goodness' sake! How ridiculous. Lesley's friends at Calder delighted in teasing her and calling her a snob for getting into the private school. Lesley hated the idea of the next five years in this snotty school, but she would have to make the best of it. As it happened, the next two years would turn out to be quite an adventure.

Lesley started at the grammar school in 1970. It was a very long day for her, after being so close to Calder Primary that she could walk it in ten minutes. Lesley found it hard getting up at 6 a.m. to be at the station for the 8 a.m. train to Pollockshaws. When the other children saw the new girl, with her skirt nearly down to her ankles, long grey socks and a blazer nearly down to her knees, they laughed at her and teased her mercilessly. Lesley felt thoroughly miserable; she hadn't wanted to go to this school and there was no way she wanted to be friends with these snobby bitches. Pam insisted that Lesley should wear her hair in pigtails to keep it tidy during the day. This made her look even more ridiculous. The other new girls had the latest hairstyles and they wore tights, not ridiculous long socks. Their shoes were smart but fashionable. Lesley felt like a freak compared to them.

She did grow to enjoy the independence of being able to leave the house early to catch the train. She loved arriving home later, although she found it difficult trying to juggle housework with homework. Lesley wasn't quite sure how she would be able to cope with the high standards of homework required for school, whilst trying to avoid a beating at home for not completing all her chores on time. Pam found it harder to pick on Lesley as her own children were getting older and demanded more of her attention. However, she did find a way to inflict the ultimate humiliation on Lesley. Every morning, Pam would inspect the parting at the back of Lesley's head, checking her pigtails were evenly matched. Every morning, despite Lesley's best efforts, Pam would tear the hairbands out of her hair and scrape the comb down the middle of Lesley's head, like a knife, before pulling her hair so hard that she feared it would come out. Eventually Pam warned Lesley that unless she got her parting straight every day for the next two weeks, she would have to have her hair cut short. Lesley tried her best every day. She did her parting, then contorted her body round so that she could see the back of her head in the mirror. Lesley had hated having short hair for years, so she had been thrilled when Pam said she could grow it, as long as it was tidy. She wasn't about to have it all cut off.

Sadly, Pam had other ideas. She knew how to humiliate and upset this girl. One morning, after the two week trial had expired, Lesley did her hair as usual. She had asked a couple of the girls she liked at school, how they did their hair. The girls said their mum helped them. What I would give to have a proper mum again, Lesley thought. And so it was that on this particular morning, Pam was in a particularly foul mood. 'Haircut for you tonight,' she barked at Lesley. Lesley didn't like the sound of that. She had been subjected to Pam's 'haircuts' before and she knew that she was no hair stylist. Lesley confided in her friend Ann at school. She told her how Pam and Nuri beat her and how Pam had threatened to cut her hair.

Ann was very sympathetic. 'My mum died,' she said, 'but we have a housekeeper. She doesn't treat me like that woman treats you.' Lesley felt a bit better. Ann seemed to understand.

Lesley went home from school that day, dreading what the evening would bring her. The evening meal went off without event and Lesley completed the washing and drying up, made the sandwiches and was just about to go upstairs to do her homework, when Pam appeared, scissors in hand. She pulled a chair away from the dining table and placed it in the middle of the kitchen floor. Lesley's heart sank. She knew that her lovely long hair was about to disappear.

Pam instructed her to sit on the chair. Lesley tried to plead, in the vain hope that she might be granted a reprieve. Not a hope. Instead of untying her hair first then cutting it, Pam cut her hair, straight across the pigtails. Tears stung Lesley's eyes as she watched her beautiful long dark hair hit the floor, still tied up in pigtails. Not content, Pam proceeded to cut more hair from her head. Lesley thought she must surely be nearly bald by now.

'That's better,' Pam said. 'No excuses not to look tidy now.' Lesley was crying but Pam showed no emotion. She instructed Lesley to sweep her hair up, throw it away and put the chair back.

Lesley cried buckets as she looked at her lovely long hair lying on the floor. She cried a lot more when she eventually went upstairs and looked in the mirror. She looked like a boy again. Oh no! That meant tomorrow the kids would be even more horrible to her than usual. Maybe if she ran away she could say she was a boy, which might help her remain undetected for longer. For now though, Lesley would have to get through the next day at school. She had to cope somehow, there was going to be no hiding place for her.

The next day, Lesley was up early. She tried to make her hair look longer, but it looked ridiculous, whatever she did with it. For the first time ever, Lesley wore her hat all the way to school. Ann knew there was something wrong. Lesley hated wearing her hat and only wore it when she had to. When they got nearer to the school gates, Ann asked if anything was wrong. Lesley tearfully revealed her hair and Ann gasped in horror. She had never seen such a bad attempt at a haircut. Ann asked Lesley what she was going to do. Lesley didn't have an answer. All she could pray for was that her hair grew back, and fast.

The girls at school laughed at Lesley when they saw her hair. Girls at a private grammar school can be vile, horrid bitches when they choose to be.

They taunted her all day.

'This is a girl's school, why have we got a boy in school?'

'Miss, why have we got a boy in our class?'

Lesley wanted to kill them all, but most of all she wanted to kill Pam. Lesley's experience at the school went badly downhill after that. She hated these stuck-up kids, who all had the latest gadgets, the latest fashion, rich parents who indulged their spoilt brats. Lesley decided that she was going to play up whenever possible so that she could be removed from the school. She skipped lessons. She was rude to the children and the teachers. On the train journey there and home, Lesley and Ann had great fun shouting and shrieking and annoying everyone. Every time the train stopped, the two girls would jump off and run to the next carriage. Eventually the guards would get really annoyed and threaten to ban them from the trains in future. Lesley would deliberately miss the early train, which meant that she had to go into Glasgow Central and get the train to Motherwell from there. The less time she had to be in that horrible house, the better she liked it. Lesley loved the big station in Glasgow. It was always busy and she loved the smell of the diesel dripping from the trains.

She used to look longingly at the night train bound for London Euston, wishing that she could escape from her keepers and disappear into the hustle and bustle of London. Sadly, with no money and no friends in London, this was never going to become a reality.

Lesley stopped doing some of her homework, deliberately. After a term of this bad behaviour, a letter was sent to Pam and Nuri informing them that Lesley's behaviour was not of the standard they wished from their pupils. Lesley was given a beating, but she didn't care. She hated everyone and all she wanted to do was escape from Motherwell.

Due to Lesley's downward spiral in conduct, Pam decided that she would take over the disciplining of this wayward child. This was not a good omen for Lesley, who was growing more defiant by the day. When Lesley put her school shirts into the laundry basket for the white wash, Pam would remove them and examine the collars. If there was the slightest hint of dirt on the collar, Lesley would be marched to the bathroom to have her neck scrubbed with a scrubbing brush normally used to wash the floor. Lesley grew to hate the smell of carbolic soap. Once the ceremonial washing of the neck had been completed, Lesley was made to wash each shirt by hand. Any trace of dirt on the collar would result in it being thrown at her to wash again, until the collar was spotless.

Pam was triumphant in her humiliation of this child. 'From now on,' she said, 'I will be inspecting your shirt collar every time you have shirts to go in the wash. Is that understood?' Lesley was now really irritated and thoroughly fed up with the list of criticisms that was being added to on a daily basis. She wished that she could tell someone what was happening at home, but she knew from previous experience that nobody ever believed it could be as bad as she said it was.

Because Lesley was behaving so badly at the grammar school, Pam and Nuri decided they could not live with the shame of their family reputation being tainted. They threatened to withdraw Lesley from the private school, much to her delight. Lesley was given one final year to change her ways before she would be enrolled into Dalziel High School. The lectures about her behaviour and about how she had disgraced the family went over her head. Lesley had stopped listening a long time ago. Now all she could think about was how to murder Pam and Nuri and get away with it. She hated them with all her heart and vowed that one day the world would know what they had done to her.

The long dragging summer holidays came around again. Lesley dreaded the holidays every year. It would mean weeks of cleaning, gardening and having to look after the spoilt younger brats in the family, who were growing up to be as obnoxious as their parents. It was during this holiday that Harry and Lillian had come to stay. When they retired, they sold the shop in Harrogate and moved north, choosing a lovely little flat in St. Andrews, five minutes away from the beach. During the summer holidays, the family would go and stay in St. Andrews for a couple of weeks. The flat was tiny and tempers frayed as everyone got in each other's way.

One day, Pam asked Lesley to take Suki and Pancho to

the park for their morning walk. Pancho was now an old man and very slow on his feet. Lesley eventually reached the park and let the dogs off the lead, as she always did. They were both gentle animals who wouldn't hurt anybody. Suddenly, Pancho collapsed on the grass, refusing to get up. Lesley was baffled; she had no idea what was going on. She knelt down beside him crying and begging him to get up, but he just lay there. Suki came over and nuzzled him, but the old boy could not move. In a panic and sobbing loudly, Lesley took Suki and ran back to the flat. She burst into the kitchen and started trying to explain what had happened to Pancho. Pam ran back to the park with her, but it was too late. Pancho had died.

Of course, Lesley got the blame for the dog's death. Who else's fault could it be that the dog was old and his heart had given out? Lesley was dragged back to the flat and shut in her room for the day, trying to understand how she could possibly have killed the dog, when all she had done was to take him for a walk. Lesley hated St. Andrews after that day.

The following year, Harry's chain-smoking caught up with him and he had become very ill. He struggled to breathe, but Lesley had no sympathy for him, she had always hated the stench of cigarettes around him. That said, she didn't like the way Pam shouted at him; it seemed so cruel when he was her father and clearly seriously ill. One night, there was a great commotion in the bedroom next to Lesley's, where Harry and Lillian were sleeping. Lesley felt very irritated by the disturbance. She was tired and wanted a decent sleep so that she would be fresh the next day. There was much bumping about, then some shouting before everything went quiet. In the morning, Lesley discovered that Harry had died in the night. To her horror, his dead body was in the bedroom next to hers, which terrified her. Lesley had never experienced death in this way, as she and her sister had been removed from the family home at the time of her father's death. She found the thought of a dead body in the next room almost too much to cope with. According to Baha'i law, the body must be washed with rose water and wrapped in a rubber cloth to protect it from decay. The undertaker must make the coffin and bring it to the house; the body cannot be removed.

Lesley had just about got her head around this concept when, one morning, Pam told her to go into the room and fetch some clean sheets out of the chest of drawers. Lesley was petrified! She had never seen a corpse before and the thought terrified her. She resolved to delay following this instruction in the hope that Pam would go and get the sheets herself. The morning continued, until Pam asked Lesley if she had collected the sheets from the front bedroom. Lesley knew she would be in trouble, but she really couldn't face being in the same room as a dead body. She explained to Pam that she was afraid because Granddad Harry was lying there dead and she was frightened to be in the room alone with his body. Pam was furious. She dragged Lesley upstairs and pushed her into the bedroom, barking at her to get the sheets from the drawer. Lesley tried to resist but Pam delivered a hefty punch to her back and she flew through the door, almost landing on the bed that Granddad Harry was laid out on! Lesley let out a scream then ran to the drawer and fetched the sheets. On her way out, she quickly looked at Granddad Harry, half-expecting his eyes to open, or him to sit up and start speaking to her. This was a terrifying experience for any child and Lesley would never forget this incident.

Eventually, the day of the funeral arrived and people

seemed to descend on the house from all over the country. Baha'i funerals are a celebration of life, not a mourning of the deceased.

Lesley was overwhelmed when people kept arriving at the house. The car arrived, along with Granddad Harry in his coffin. Lesley was bemused by all the fuss. The car journey to the cemetery seemed to go on and on. The cemetery was on the other side of Glasgow and it seemed to take an age to get there. Everybody filed into the little hall for the service. Lesley started to cry. She had seen Granddad Harry lying dead, wrapped in a rubber sheet. Now he was in a wooden box which was going to be put in the ground. It was all too much for her little mind to deal with. She thought back to Raymond's death, her beloved daddy. Did they put him in a box too?

Suddenly Lesley realised that she didn't even know when her daddy's funeral had taken place, or who was there and where was he buried? She cried some more tears.

From nowhere, a fist came down on her leg and a voice whispered through gritted teeth, 'Shut up, you stupid bitch! What are you crying for?'

Lesley looked up at Pam and thought how grotesque she looked – so ugly and so unkind. Lesley vowed that one day she would expose her for the monster she was. She tried really hard not to cry, but that made things worse and she cried more, not least because her leg was stinging from the punch she had received.

Once the service was over, everyone filed into the graveyard and prayers were said before the coffin was lowered into the ground. Lillian was distraught, but Pam made no effort to console her mother. Lesley thought that Pam must not have a soul; she had no time or affection for anyone, only herself.

When all was done, the guests drifted off to wherever they had come from and a very sad Lillian was bundled back into the car to return to Motherwell with the family. Lesley tried to console her, but Pam slapped her away, telling her that Lillian was perfectly fine and didn't need the fuss. Looking at Lillian that day, Lesley wondered once more how such a sweet lady could have given birth to such a vile monster.

Life returned to normal, but Lillian did not return home to St. Andrews. She continued to stay with the family for some considerable time, until Pam constantly yelling at her, and the rest of the family, drove her away.

Chapter 11

A Change of Plan

———◦⊙◦———

By now, Lesley had started to develop breasts, like every girl of her age. She was still wearing the old-fashioned woollen vests that Pam had bought for her and she was very conscious of the little bumps underneath her tops. Her friends at school seemed way in advance of her and she envied them, all wearing pretty bras under their school shirts.

Lesley aged twelve.

Lesley decided that she needed to ask for a bra before she returned to school for the new term. She tried to choose her timing very carefully to be sure Pam was in a good mood before she asked the question. She waited until they were alone in the dining room one afternoon.

'I have been thinking,' Lesley began.

'Oh really?' Pam had that patronising sneer in her voice that told Lesley she didn't want to listen.

Lesley continued, choosing her words very carefully. 'I seem to be getting bigger around the bust and I wondered whether I might be able to wear a bra. All my friends are wearing bras, and I feel stupid wearing a vest.'

Pam looked up from her book and eyed Lesley up and down. 'Lift your top,' she instructed. Lesley lifted her top to reveal the two little mounds that were fast developing underneath her vest. 'You're right,' Pam said. 'I will take you and get you measured for a bra.'

Lesley was amazed. Pam never did anything without a fight. The next week, when it was time to go and buy her new school uniform, Lesley was excited. She was going to become a grown-up and wear a bra and have periods like all her friends. Her periods were proving an insurmountable monthly obstacle. Her sanitary belt did not fit properly and she was always having accidents. Her friends laughed at her when she explained about the sanitary belt. Their mums made sure they had tampons or stick-on sanitary towels, not the cumbersome things that Lesley was forced to use. Every time Lesley had an accident, she would be made to wash her underwear by hand, scrubbing till every last trace of blood was gone. To make matters worse, Lesley was expected to buy her own sanitary towels with her pocket money. However, as Pam always found excuses why she had not earned her pocket money, Lesley frequently had to use toilet paper instead of sanitary towels, which was extremely humiliating for a growing girl.

The day of the bra shopping arrived. Pam took Lesley, Lucy and John into Glasgow to a big department store. The assistant measured Lesley's bust and confirmed the size of bra required for her. Lesley spotted a very pretty white lacy bra hanging up. She went over and picked it up.

'You can put that back. Those bras are for common sluts!' a voice said from behind her. Lesley's sense of foreboding grew. What terrible monstrosity of a bra was she going to have to wear? Pam was talking to the shop assistant. The lady went away and came back with an old-fashioned, shapeless, ugly bra. Lesley had never seen anything like it in her life!

'What's that?' she asked the lady.

'This, my dear, is what your mum says you need for school.'

The lady felt sorry for Lesley. Usually, the mums would come in and let their daughters choose a pretty bra to start them on the journey to womanhood. She didn't much like this domineering woman who was obviously going to force this child to wear a bra designed in the 1940s.

'Here we are,' Pam said. 'That's better. Much more suitable for school wear.'

Lesley was absolutely mortified. She couldn't wear this ridiculous thing, the children would ridicule her even more than they did already! Pam instructed her to go and try it on. Lesley put the stupid bra on. It was made of cotton; there was not a hint of lace and the straps seemed to go on forever. Lesley adjusted the straps to fit her skinny frame, put her top on and exited the cubicle, trying not to cry. 'Let's have a look,' Pam said. 'And where, might I ask, is your vest?'

Lesley had deliberately not put the vest back on. Her friends at school didn't wear vests; they were for children and old people. Lesley lamely held out the vest. 'Well, I suggest you go and put it on. Decent girls don't show everything they've got to the world,' Pam said crossly. Lesley wandered back into the cubicle, feeling utterly helpless in this situation. She put the vest on over the bra and shed a tear as she looked in the cubicle mirror and realised how completely outdated and stupid she looked. She went back to join the others and Pam paid for the bra.

Next came the school uniform. As with every year, the shirts were two sizes too big, so the collars gaped and

Lesley's tie wouldn't sit properly. Her skirt was way below her knees, but that was manageable as she could hoist it up at the waistband to shorten it, once she was out of sight of the house. Her jumper was so big that the sleeves hung a long way over the ends of her little short arms. Lesley folded them once, twice, third time lucky.

Lesley thought that it was about time she should be allowed to wear tights, like all the other girls. She was the only one forced to wear long grey socks to school. She knew she looked ridiculous so she decided that as Pam had already humiliated her with the bra she would go all out to get as far up her nose as she could. She asked politely if she could have some tights, as she was the only girl in her year still in socks.

Pam was not amused. This girl was growing up way too fast. However, she felt that in the circumstances it would be the ideal time to try her with tights and see how she coped with them. When she agreed, Lesley was very excited. Now she could be a grown-up girl, like all the other girls, and not have to feel like the freak of the class. Lesley thought that her jumper and blazer would cover up the bra and vest, so she felt happier.

The last item on the list was the shoes. No fashionable, pretty shoes like all her friends had. Lesley's shoes were always too small and the most ridiculous style that Pam could find. Lesley longed for the day when she could buy her own clothes and shoes. She vowed that nobody would ever make her look ridiculous when she was grown-up.

The new school term started and Lesley returned to the grammar school for her second year, hating every minute there. She was rude to the staff and rude to her classmates. Once again she played havoc on the trains with her friend Ann. She was fast becoming a proper rebel and enjoying every minute of it. The beatings and tellings-off no longer worried Lesley; she was determined not to be beaten into submission by these monsters in the house.

The younger children were growing up and realising that getting Lesley into trouble was great fun, when they didn't have to take the punishment. Lesley thought that they were horrid. She didn't try too hard to conceal her contempt for them. The girls at the grammar school were from wealthy families, so their holidays were always abroad and their clothes always smart. They treated Lesley like a peasant, laughing at her clothes and ridiculing her hair. Lesley hated everyone and wished they could all be drowned in the River Clyde.

The end of the school year came around again and Lesley waited for her lecture. Sure enough, it wasn't long in coming. Lesley had heard it all before, so she wasn't the least bit bothered. All she wanted was to get to Dalziel and be with her friends from primary school. Pam was full of herself. Every insult she could think of she used against Lesley. Pam told her she was thick, she was stupid, she was a useless slut who would have six children and no husband by the time she was thirty.

Lesley laughed inwardly, her inner self whispering obscenities at this stupid woman, who wasn't even her mother, laying down the law and calling her names. Lesley half listened to this demented creature in front of her shouting and ranting. She vowed that she would prove them wrong. She would never have six children – she hated children after having to babysit all the children at every Baha'i meeting. She would work all her life and have nice clothes and nice holidays. She would show them. The next term would be a bit different, but Lesley really wanted to meet up with some of her old school friends. She would have another year to wait before she finally got to mix with children she actually liked.

The summer holidays were long and very trying for a young girl whose hormones were playing havoc. Lesley tried her best to stay out of the way. She hid in the garden and did some weeding. She took the children to the park and played till they cried to go home. She pretended to study hard, burying her head in any book she could get her hands on. She thought it very odd that two very religious people had *Lady Chatterley's Lover* on the bookshelf. When Pam and Nuri were not around, Lesley would read a bit of the book. There were words in there she had never heard of! She didn't know what they meant but she was sure they were very rude.

Lesley turned fourteen during the summer holidays. Now a truly feisty teenager, she had long since grown tired of the constant abuse and trying to hide bruises and scratches from any visitors. Once more, the customary buying of the largest clothing and the most ridiculous skirts was completed. However, Pam was determined to make Lesley pay for getting herself removed from the prestigious grammar school. Lesley asked for a new school blazer. She admired the Dalziel High uniform and the blazer was a lovely shade of royal blue.

Pam thought differently. She insisted that Lesley wear her blazer from Hutchesons' Grammar, which was a different shade of blue and made of wool, not acrylic. Lesley was made to stitch the Dalziel crest onto the old blazer. On her first day at Dalziel High School, the form mistress was less than impressed. Lesley was told that she must have a Dalziel blazer. That night, she went home and told Pam about the instruction from her form mistress. Pam was not swayed. She said that Lesley had humiliated the family by getting herself removed from the grammar school, so her punishment would be to wear the blazer as a reminder of the failure and the disgrace she had brought on the family. The next day, Lesley returned to the school and explained to the form mistress what Pam had said. This was met with fury and a letter sent to Pam, advising her that Lesley would be allowed to get away with wearing the wrong blazer, but only for one year. The pupils teased Lesley about her blazer but she didn't take any notice; she was happy just being at Dalziel amongst people she knew from primary.

She settled in and enjoyed going to school. No more having to get up at 6 a.m., no more long train journeys in carriages stinking of cigarette smoke. This was a whole new experience.

Pam now worked at Hamilton Academy as head of the domestic science department. She had been driving for

'Dalziel High, where Lesley would ultimately find the companionship and courage to help her survive.'

some time and she and Nuri had invested in a camper van. Lesley hated it. It was a horrible light blue Transit camper van, with a canvas roof that lifted up to reveal two bunk beds. Lesley was expected to leave Dalziel High School and exit via Hamilton Road, which is the main road between Motherwell and Hamilton. However, Lesley hated having to go home in the blue monstrosity, which was no good for her reputation, so she used to sneak out the back way and dawdle up Crawford Street. Her friends used to joke that the Grim Reaper was waiting outside the gates for her. Pam used to wait, but Lesley made sure she was one of the last out of school, so that she could not be seen. When Lesley got home, there was an inquest as to why she hadn't been there to be picked up. Lesley wanted to tell Pam exactly why she wasn't there, but she dreaded the response, so she made up stories about the teacher wanting to discuss her homework, or having to put the lesson materials away. After a while, Pam gave up and went straight home. She didn't believe the girl but thought that if she was stupid enough to want to walk all the way home, that was her look out. Lesley on the other hand, thoroughly enjoyed the walk home.

It was during the spring of 1972, after Lesley had run away yet again, that Banoo and Rustom came to live in Hamilton. They were renting a poky little flat in Cadzow Street, and Lesley thought it was an awful place. It was like one of the old-fashioned tenement buildings. The stairs and the walls were concrete and the passageways smelt of urine. Lesley felt sorry for her grandparents. Banoo and Rustom explained that Pam and Nuri thought it would be a good idea if they moved to Scotland to be near Lesley, as she had said all along that was her dream, to be reunited with her grandparents. The deal was that if Lesley had done all her chores she would be allowed to go there on a Saturday and stay till Sunday evening. Lesley loved that idea, but it was not going to turn out the way she hoped.

The first few weeks were great. Lesley would pack up her nightclothes and clothes for the next day, then she would be allowed to go for the bus. However, a full inspection of the house had to be done first, to make sure that all surfaces were dust free and all her homework was done. Lesley loved going to stay with her grandparents. It was just like the holiday she had spent with them in Hove, all those years ago. Banoo would allow Lesley to go to the shops to buy her groceries and Rustom allowed her to browse through the many books he had on his bookshelf. They also gave Lesley some money, which they said she was to spend on herself. Lesley would set out on a Saturday afternoon, purse in hand, looking for some small item that she could treat herself to and hide away, in case Pam saw it and threw it away.

Lesley bought some deodorant; she knew the girls at school were using it. She carefully unscrewed the tops and smelt the lovely scents of all the deodorants, eventually settling on one like her friend had at school. She bought some new tights as hers were always ripping and laddering and Pam would force her to repair them carefully, which made them look stupid. Looking stupid was something Lesley was very used to.

Rustom told Lesley that if she ran away again, they would move away from Hamilton and she would not see them again. Lesley carefully dusted and hoovered everywhere on Saturday mornings and put her washing away neatly in the wardrobe. She completed her homework and put her books back in her satchel. She was determined that she was going to stay with her grandparents.

Pam was very spiteful and did not like the fact that Lesley adored her grandparents. Wherever possible, she would make an excuse why Lesley could not go to stay with her them. One Saturday, Lesley had got herself ready and left to get the bus. She rushed up the stairs to her grandparents' flat. She hadn't been there an hour when the telephone rang.

Rustom looked serious. 'It's Pam for you, darling,' he said to Lesley.

Her little heart sank. What did the bitch want now? She gingerly picked up the receiver. 'Hello?' she said quietly.

That all-too-familiar spiteful voice was on the other end. 'Get the next bus back here,' she barked.

'Why?' Lesley asked, not liking the sound of this.

'You didn't do the dusting properly, so you will return home to complete it.'

Lesley was furious. She knew she had done the dusting properly and she could not understand where Pam had found any dust.

'Do you hear me, girl? The next bus.' The line went dead.

Lesley was shaking, with fear and with rage. 'I have to go, Granddad,' she said. 'If I don't go, she'll beat me again.'

Her grandfather came and put his arms round her. He was fed up with Lesley telling him about how many slaps and beatings she had been dealt during the week, but he felt powerless to have any influence over Pam and Nuri. After all, they were her legal guardians. Lesley deliberately didn't pack up all her belongings. Rustom gave her the money for the bus back to Motherwell and she set off, her heart firmly in her mouth. She walked ever so slowly from the bus stop to the house. When she arrived, she slammed the door shut in fury, then went to find Pam. 'I'm back.

Where is this dust I missed?' Lesley spoke with venom in her voice. She knew that Pam had done this deliberately to ruin her weekend. Besides, who else uses their children like housekeeping staff? Pam took Lesley through to the hallway. She walked half way up the stairs, then stopped. She bent down and ran her finger along the skirting that framed the stairs. Gloating that she had found fault, Pam rammed her finger into Lesley's face. Lesley looked at the finger, then at Pam, then back at the skirting board. Trying not to show her contempt for this creature was getting harder and harder for Lesley, and dragging her away from the two people she loved more than anyone else in the world was a very bad move. She looked at Pam. 'Well, now you've scraped the dust off there, I won't have to do it, will I?' As soon as the words came out of her mouth, she wanted to push them back in again, but it was too late.

Pam was seething with rage. 'How dare you!' she shouted and with a swift push of the hand, Lesley found herself tumbling through the air, down the stairs to the hallway below. Pam followed her down, giving her a hefty kick as she stormed through to the kitchen. Lesley was crying, tears of pain from the fall, but also tears of rage. That woman had made her come all the way back for a one inch area of dust she had missed. How Lesley hated her. She had never felt so much hate for anyone in her life as she felt for this woman. She vowed that she would get her revenge somehow.

Lesley sat for a few minutes, checking that all her limbs still moved and she hadn't broken anything in the fall. Her head hurt, but her heart hurt more. She went back to the kitchen and said, 'I'm going back to Granddad's now.' She opened the door, waiting for someone to shout at her to stop, or for someone to come after her, but nothing happened. Lesley slowly walked back to the bus.

It was a very sore little girl that arrived back at Rustom and Banoo's home in the afternoon. They questioned her about what had happened and she explained about being pushed down the stairs. Rustom and Banoo were furious but, as always, they had to keep quiet. They bitterly regretted ever allowing Pam and Nuri anywhere near their darling granddaughter. Lesley seriously wished that she could report them and get them sent to jail, but she had no idea where to start.

Lesley had found a good friend at Dalziel High, called Margo. The girls were in Douglas house. Janice was another girl who got picked on by the other children and Lesley used to spend some lunchtimes with her, walking up Airbles Road to Elvan Tower, so that Janice could check on her mother, who was in poor health. Lesley had a small group of friends as most of the children thought she was a freak, with her boy's haircut, clothes that didn't fit and ridiculous shoes and this weird religion she belonged to.

Margo was different; she felt sorry for Lesley. Margo was a very pretty girl, with beautiful long blonde hair. How Lesley wished she could have hair like that, without it being chopped off every time it grew. Margo was an only child and a bit of a rebel, always up to mischief. Lesley was too afraid to get into any mischief, lest the teachers phone Pam and tell her what she had done.

Lesley decided to confess to Margo what was going on at home. Nobody could ever understand why Lesley's clothes were all the wrong sizes, why she had such old-fashioned shoes, why she never had the right equipment for lessons. Lesley shared with Margo how she had been the object of ridicule all the way through primary and secondary school.

Margo and Lesley used to spend their lunchtimes together. They went to the chip shop or to Auld's Bakery in Brandon Parade, to buy a sausage roll or pasty, or to the sweet shop, instead of having a proper lunch. Lesley really liked Margo; she was easy to talk to and didn't go blabbing to the other children about what was going on in her life. One day, after a particularly bad beating, Lesley showed Margo the bruises on her back. Margo was horrified. She asked Lesley if there was anyone she could tell. Lesley explained that her grandparents were powerless to do anything, but they had given her Uncle Roy's address. Margo suggested writing to Uncle Roy; perhaps he could help her.

Margo took Lesley home to her house some lunchtimes and it was there that Lesley would sit and write her letters to Uncle Roy. He would send the replies to Margo and she would bring the letters to school to give to Lesley. Lesley had to make sure she gave Margo the letters back the same day, in case Pam found them in her school bag. Uncle Roy also sent money to Lesley, to buy herself tights or deodorant, or just some sweets if she wanted them.

Margo's house was lovely. It was warm and welcoming, not like Lesley's prison-cell bedroom in Jerviston Street. Margo's mum was welcoming too. Margo had lovely fitted wardrobes in her bedroom, not like the old-fashioned cumbersome thing in Lesley's room. Lesley thought Margo was very lucky to have such lovely parents.

Margo also had a key and could come and go as she pleased. She had nice clothes and perfume and makeup. Lesley could never imagine that she would be allowed such things. Margo gave Lesley a deodorant to take home with her. Lesley had to be very careful. If she was found in possession of such an item, the consequences were always the same – a good old beating with the riding crop.

Margo's house felt like a safe haven to Lesley. She wished she could live in a nice house with normal parents. This place was a far cry from where she was living. Despite Lesley being able to visit her grandparents as and when it suited Pam and Nuri, Lesley knew that she would never be happy till she could escape from Motherwell and from that horrible house. She was still writing to Uncle Roy and detailing all the beatings: how often, the dates, what she was beaten for. Pam was still insulting her on a daily basis. There were never any compliments or hugs, never any praise, no matter how well she did at school. Lesley felt numb. She didn't want to get old if this was all that life had to offer. It was far too much like hard work.

Term ended and Margo wished Lesley all the best for the holidays. Margo was lucky. Her parents took her on nice holidays to Blackpool or to Torquay. She was allowed to go out on her own and go into shops on her own. Lesley's stomach turned over as she thought of the long holiday ahead and all the beatings she had to look forward to. Lesley had been hiding the money Uncle Roy had sent her. She used to hide it in her bedroom, underneath the wardrobe, or under the bookcase. Lesley was still determined to get away from that house, somehow.

The summer holiday started and Lesley was not allowed to visit her grandparents. There was always an excuse, Lesley lost count of the excuses, but it made her more determined to escape this hell. Enough was enough.

One morning, Pam had taken Lucy and John out to town. Lesley seized her opportunity. She bundled some clothes into a bag, along with a hat – that would make her harder to recognise. Off she went, heading for the station. Lesley had a plan in her head. If she could reach Glasgow Central, she might have enough money to get a ticket to

London, where nobody would ever find her again. She ran all the way to the station and bought a single ticket for Glasgow Central. She sat on the platform, hoping that nobody would come along that recognised her. Eventually the train pulled in and Lesley jumped on board. She felt so grown-up, sitting in the carriage, gazing out of the window without a care in the world. As soon as the train reached Glasgow, Lesley headed to the ladies toilet, where she changed her clothes and pulled her hat on to hide her dark hair. Lesley bought herself a bar of chocolate and a packet of crisps from the kiosk on the station; she would need some food to keep her going on her journey.

Lesley exited the station and set off in the direction she knew, which would take her to the motorway. She figured she would be able to hitch a lift with one of the lorry drivers going south. She followed the signs for the motorway, carefully picking her way amongst the passers-by without attracting any attention. She figured she could get a long way before anyone had even missed her. Lesley was getting nearer to sixteen, which would mean she could legally leave the horrible house and be free of Pam and Nuri. She skipped along the road, feeling a real sense of freedom.

Suddenly, she heard sirens. Was it the police looking for her again? Surely not. She breathed a sigh of relief as an ambulance flew over the crossroads in front of her. Lesley carried on walking, but she was lost now. The motorway seemed to have got further away and she had no idea where she was. She heard sirens again, so she ran down to the riverbank and hid under a bridge till they had passed by.

Suddenly, she heard a shout. 'There she is! Down there!' A big burly policeman was coming towards her. Lesley turned to run the other way, but another policeman was coming in the opposite direction. The first policeman grabbed her arm and Lesley tried her hardest to wriggle free, but he wasn't going to let go in a hurry. 'Oh no you don't, young lady,' the policeman said. He walked Lesley back to the main road, still keeping a firm hold of her arm. The policeman opened the door to the police car and signalled Lesley to get into the back seat. She climbed into the car, tired and utterly miserable. She had failed in her bid to escape again. 'Cat got your tongue girl?' the policeman asked sarcastically.

Lesley was furious. She was furious with herself that her escape attempt had been foiled again. She was furious that they had found her. She was furious that she now had to go back and endure another beating. Why would nobody believe her when she told them how bad her life was in that awful house? Lesley wanted to scream. She couldn't wait for her sixteenth birthday to come around.

She sat quietly in the police car for a few minutes. Then she spoke to the policeman. 'Do you have any children?' she asked him.

'Yes, I do. I have two children,' came the reply.

'Do you beat them?' Lesley asked him.

'Good God, child. Why would I do that?' The policeman was shocked by this question.

Lesley carried on. 'Do you know why I keep running away?' she asked him.

'I have no idea, my girl,' he replied.

Lesley explained that these people— no, she corrected herself, not people, monsters, beat her every day, how Pam had thrown her down the stairs, how she had so cruelly cut her hair to make Lesley look like a boy.

The policeman was not shocked. This was the 1970s. There were no hard and fast rules about discipline in the home. Lesley told the policeman about her childhood; she told him everything she could remember. 'Please, please,

I'm begging you, don't take me back there.' Lesley was desperate. 'I would rather go to the workhouse. Please don't take me back there'.

The policeman smiled kindly at her in the mirror. 'Believe me, young lady, the workhouse is no place for a respectable lass like you. I'm sure it's not that bad. You're just upset because you've been told off at home. I see it all the time.' Lesley wasn't sure how she felt just at that moment. She felt desolate, abandoned. Nobody ever believed what she told them. She just wanted to die. She buried her face in her hands and cried and cried, all the way back to Motherwell.

Chapter 12

The Rescue Plan

———— ·❦· ————

Lesley knew what would be waiting for her when she got back to Jerviston Street. The same old lecture about her being useless, a slut, she belonged in the workhouse, ungrateful bitch … She had heard it so many times, she could give herself the lecture! One thing she did know, she had to leave or she had to die.

The car pulled up outside the front door. Pam was waiting. Lesley's heart sank. As soon as the policeman left the house, she knew what would happen next. There were the usual pleasantries, the thank you to the police for finding her and the crocodile tears, pretending to be so worried. Lesley wasn't fooled. She'd seen it too many times before. Actually, she thought, Pam should be on the stage – she was such a good actress. Nuri was waiting, riding crop in his hand. Lesley had already decided she wasn't going to hold back. This time they could have a taste of their own medicine and if she was going to get a beating, she might as well make it worth it. She waited to be summoned forward for her beating.

'Just before you do this' she said, 'I just want you to know I hate you both. I really, really hate you both.' She pulled her pants down and laid over the bed, saying the same words over and over as each lash of the riding crop hit her flesh. Lesley knew she had gone too far, but it was too late and anyway, and she did hate them, so she was only telling the truth. All the long, hard years of beatings, of being punched, kicked, having her hair pulled, Lesley had now reached the point of no return. She was told there would be no evening meal for her, so she got ready for bed and lay in her room, contemplating her next great escape.

The rest of the holiday passed without too much hassle. There was the odd slap and an occasional beating, but Lesley knew that wasn't an end to them; it was just a lull in the storm. Her fifteenth birthday arrived and Lesley waited for the usual lacklustre presents. No nice smellies, no pretty, fashionable clothes, no jewellery. There was a new dressing gown, some pens and pencils and some frumpy clothes. Lesley was less than excited.

Just after her birthday, Pam summoned her to the kitchen and told her to sit down. Lesley sat down nervously, never taking her eyes off Pam's hands. She knew about these lectures; they usually resulted in a sly slap or punch at some point. Pam began her lecture and Lesley listened very carefully, to see what the dragon would have to say this time. 'You, young lady, are one very ungrateful little cow. We took you in when your own mother didn't want you and if it wasn't for us, you would be out on the street. We have tried very hard to give you a decent home and bring you up to be a decent human being. You have repaid our kindness by lying, running away multiple times, making up stories about us being horrible, cruel people. We have decided that as you think you are so clever and so wonderful, you can leave this house when you are sixteen and make your own way in life.' Lesley breathed a sigh of relief. At least she knew now that she could leave when she was sixteen and they couldn't and wouldn't stop her leaving. Lesley thought this was the best thing she had heard in ages.

Pam hadn't finished. 'As you chose to run away, yet

again, your grandparents have been informed of this and they have decided to move away. The whole point of them being here was to support you, but you have let them down. They are moving at the weekend and you won't see them again.' Lesley had kind of worked out that something was going on with her grandparents. Anyway, she figured her dad had killed himself and abandoned her and Karen, her mum had abandoned her and Karen, so what did it matter if her grandparents did the same? Pam was still talking, so Lesley focussed her energy into listening. 'Your chores will be slightly reduced from now on. You will do your own washing, by hand, every weekend, except for your towels and bedding, which can go in the machine. You will do your own ironing and make sure your school uniform and shoes are clean and tidy ready for Monday mornings. Is that clear?' Lesley nodded. Shouldn't be too difficult to do that, she thought.

Lesley retreated to her bedroom and thought about what she would do when she was sixteen. She was going to get as far away from these monsters as she could – that was a priority. She would find her grandparents and apologise for messing them around; that was also very important to her. She would also find Karen, as she had no idea where she might be either.

Lesley found it hard to do all the chores, even though there were less of them, and do her washing and ironing in timely fashion. She was washing her clothes in the kitchen one night when Simon came into the room. He was over six feet tall, not at all handsome and a bit of a recluse that only joined the family at mealtimes. He sat down on a kitchen chair and unzipped his trousers. From within he exposed a huge erection. Lesley had never seen such a thing before, she didn't even know what it was! She carried on with the washing, determined not to have anything to do with whatever Simon was doing. He called her over, but fear would not allow her to move so she carried on with her washing. Again he called her over and again she refused. 'If you don't do what I want you to, I will tell Pam that you smashed a plate and you'll be in big trouble!' he said menacingly. Lesley looked at him. Just looking at him made her feel sick, but what was he doing with that thing in his hand, rubbing it up and down? She gingerly walked across the kitchen. 'That's better,' he said. 'Now, when I tell you, you put your mouth over the end and lick it.'

Lesley was mortified. She didn't like the sound of that at all. Besides, it smelt funny and her stomach turned as she thought of what she was expected to do. Simon rubbed the erection harder and faster, and then he said, 'Now.' Lesley bent her head forward, but she couldn't do what had been asked of her. She ran to the sink to be sick. Simon laughed and mopped up the mess with a tissue. He zipped his trousers back up.

Lesley was afraid; would he carry out his threat? 'Please don't say I broke a plate. I haven't done anything and I get enough beatings as it is,' she pleaded.

'I'll see how I feel about that,' Simon said.

The same sick scenario was repeated several times, until Lesley threatened to tell Pam what he was doing. It stopped abruptly at that point. Lesley had never liked this strange boy. He had no friends and was a loner, not helped by the fact that he was cruel and very spiteful. Lesley decided that when she left this house, she never wanted to see any of them ever again.

A few weeks later, the whole family was invited to a friend's birthday party. Lesley was surprised that she was going too. Usually, she was expected to stay at home and do her homework, or look after Lucy and John. Remembering her faux pas at her friend's birthday party as a child, Lesley was very careful to choose the correct people to mingle with and the correct things to say. Lesley found a lady sat on her own with a cute little baby on her lap. The baby was gorgeous, with a mop of blonde, curly hair and beautiful blue eyes. The mother looked quite young, but she had a sad, faraway look in her eyes. She had no wedding band on her finger. Lesley was very naïve about sex and reproduction. She asked if she could hold the little bundle of joy. She thought that if she ever had a child, she would love it to look like this gorgeous little one.

The party ended and everyone left to go home. On the way home in the car, Lesley mentioned that she had held the baby and how cute she was. To her complete surprise, Pam informed her that her behaviour was wholly inappropriate and this would be dealt with when they got home. Lesley's heart sank. What now? All she had done was cuddle a baby. Was that such a dreadful crime as well?

Once in the house, Pam took Lesley to her bedroom. Lesley was fully expecting a beating but instead, Pam sat her down. 'Do you know what rape means?' she asked Lesley. Lesley shook her head; she had never even heard this word. Pam continued, 'Rape is when a man forces a woman to have sex when she doesn't want to.' Lesley was puzzled; she didn't even know what sex was, never mind rape. 'Anyway, that baby was the product of a rape,' Pam concluded.

Lesley wanted to ask more questions, but she knew better than to push her luck, so she muttered quietly, 'Sorry, I didn't know.' Lesley never did quite get to grips why cuddling a baby could be such a crime. It wasn't the baby's fault.

It was during this year that Uncle Roy came to visit. He had heard from Banoo and Rustom about Lesley running away and various snippets about the beatings. He arrived by train and stayed at a hotel in Hamilton. Lesley was amazed that she was allowed to go and see him. Pam dropped her off and said she would pick her up outside the hotel later. Lesley was very excited. She hadn't seen Uncle Roy for years, though of course he had kindly been sending her money to help her.

Lesley met Uncle Roy on the steps of his hotel. He gave her a big hug. 'Where would you like to go?' he asked. Lesley directed him around the town to a coffee shop and they sat down, chattering all the while. Lesley told Uncle Roy all about Margo and how she was sneaking the letters to and from Lesley, so as not to arouse suspicion in the house of hell.

Uncle Roy was very interested to learn all about Lesley's life at school and what subjects she enjoyed the most. All too soon it was time for him to leave, but not before he had given Lesley £50 to hide away. How she would welcome that money over the next few months.

Before Lesley returned to school after the summer holidays, Pam insisted that she should wash her blazer as it was now rather grubby after being worn since Lesley had started at Hutchesons' Grammar. Lesley asked Pam how she should wash the blazer. Pam said it could go in the washing machine, on a normal dark wash. Lesley had not chosen domestic science as one of her subjects. She did not feel the need to question Pam's advice. After all, she should know which wash cycle was correct for wool.

Lesley put her blazer into the washing machine with the dark colours and Pam turned it on. To her absolute horror, when she came to put the blazer on, the whole thing had shrunk, but worst of all, the arms were now too short. Lesley begged Pam to buy her a new blazer, but her request fell on deaf ears. Pam just shrugged her shoulders and said, 'Too bad.' Lesley went back to school and was once more mercilessly teased and taunted about her ill-fitting clothes, which had now been joined by the shrunken blazer. Lesley really felt like a freak and vowed that no child of hers would ever be treated this way. Once more, Pam had succeeded in humiliating her in spectacular fashion.

Lesley worked very hard at school. She thought that if she worked hard, she could get a decent job when she left school. Lesley came home from school one day knowing that she had quite a few chores to do that evening. She wasn't quite sure how she would find time to do everything. Lesley laid the table, she emptied the dishes out of the kitchen drainer, she made all the sandwiches for the next day and she cleaned all the shoes, as she had done for many years. Unfortunately, as some of Lesley's classmates had been fooling around during lessons that afternoon, a hefty amount of homework had been set for completion the same evening.

Pam must have sensed that there was something wrong; she always seemed to know when to make more work, or pile on more criticism. 'I want you to have a bath tonight, before you go to bed,' she said. Lesley was not happy with this. Her bath nights were Monday, Wednesday and Friday. Tonight was Tuesday – why tonight? Lesley completed all the chores downstairs, then wearily retreated to her bedroom to tackle the mountain of homework. There was English, history and maths. How she hated maths! There didn't seem to be any logic to geometry and trigonometry; besides, why would she need those later in life? Lesley felt very stupid when it came to trigonometry. She just could not understand how to cope with the problems.

Lesley struggled with obtaining school equipment. Everything she needed for school had to be bought out of her own pocket money. Other children's parents were only too happy to provide their children with the necessary tools to get them through school. Lesley's bedtime was at 9 p.m. There was no way she could finish all the homework before curfew time. She plodded on through the subjects, cursing the teachers for giving so much homework.

When Lesley eventually finished, it was 10 p.m.. She put all her books away in her bag, ready for the next day. She hung her clothes up, in case Pam decided to go on the rampage in the night. Wearily, at 10.30 p.m., she climbed into bed. Lesley thought that if she were to have a bath now, she would get a beating for being late to bed. She fell into a deep sleep after a very tiring day.

She was woken by her bedroom light being switched on. Puzzled and startled, she looked at her alarm clock. It was 12.30 a.m.! All of a sudden she was yanked out of bed by the arm and thrown to the floor. Now she was fully awake. There, in all her ugliness, stood Pam. Lesley scrambled to her feet.

Pam was now stripping every part of her bed. First the sheets, then the blankets, then the mattress. 'Did you have that bath?' she asked.

Lesley knew there was no use lying. The bath was bone-dry and she hadn't used her bath towel. 'I didn't have time. it was half ten before I finished my homework tonight,' she protested.

'Never mind,' Pam said. 'You can have your bath now.'

Lesley could not believe what she was hearing. 'But it's half past twelve! And there's no hot water left!'

Pam looked coldly at her. 'So? Bath, now. I don't care if the water's cold.' She stormed out, leaving Lesley stood in the middle of the floor crying, her bed strewn all around the floor. Now she had to have a cold bath as well! This really was too much. Lesley went to the bathroom. She ran the bath. The water was freezing. The immersion tank had long since delivered up the final dregs of hot water to the last person to have a bath that night. Lesley did not relish getting into a freezing cold bath at this ungodly hour. Lesley looked at the cold water in the bath; it wasn't inviting at all. She devised a cunning plan. She carefully laid her bath towel on the floor, then splashed it with some of the freezing water. She dipped her hands in the cold water and dabbed her cheeks with it, so that she would be cold if Pam came to check that she had taken a bath. She splashed some more water onto the towel so that it would be quite wet. Then she drained the bath and cleaned it as she always did and put her towel in the airing cupboard. 'There you are you bloody cow. I had a bath, my way.'

It was now 1am. Lesley slipped her nightdress on and ran back to her bedroom to remake her bed. The sight that greeted her when she pushed the door open was not what she had expected to see. Every single piece of her clothing was the middle of the floor, along with her shoes. For one horrible moment, Lesley thought the house had been burgled, then she realised that Pam had taken revenge on her for not having a bath. Tears stung her eyes and rolled down her cheeks as she wearily put everything back where it should be, remade the bed and fell asleep.

The alarm woke her at 6.30 a.m.. Lesley was very tired in school that day. She told Margo what had happened and, as ever, Margo listened patiently and tried to calm her down. Margo invited Lesley to go to her house at lunchtime to tell her mum what had happened the night before. Margo's mum was a lovely lady. She adored her daughter and couldn't understand why anyone would want to hurt any child. Margo's mum said she would make some enquiries and let Lesley know where she could go for help. Lesley was delighted to think that she might be able to bring these monsters to account.

Lesley went home to her prison that evening, exhausted from the events of the previous night. She wondered what horrors lay in store for her tonight. She didn't have long to wait. She did her chores as usual, then went upstairs to do her homework. She settled down at her desk and started the tasks that the teachers had set. Suddenly the door burst open and Pam appeared in the doorway. Lesley wondered what was coming next. She could usually tell if trouble was brewing but this time she was caught completely unawares. Pam had a school meals dinner ticket in her hand. Lesley had forgotten to hide it away. She had been sneaking out of school with Margo at lunchtimes and getting food in town or at Margo's house before going back for the afternoon. This was a crime in Pam's eyes. She thought that only common peasant children roamed the streets at lunchtimes, because their parents couldn't afford to feed them. Lesley knew this was going to be another beating coming her way.

'Dieting, are we?' Pam asked with sarcasm oozing from every pore.

Lesley had to think fast. She put her most pitifully sad face on and replied, 'I couldn't face lunch. I felt sick where you have beaten me so many times this week.'

'Liar. You're a bloody liar!' Pam was purple in the face again. Lesley knew that face; it would haunt her forever. Pam picked Lesley's hairbrush up from her dressing table and smashed it into her face. Lesley squealed and started to cry, nursing the stinging spot where the brush had landed. Pam grabbed her hair and pulled her head back. 'You think I'm stupid, don't you, but you have been seen in town.' Lesley would dearly have loved to know who was spiteful enough to drop her in the cart, but she knew Pam would never tell her who had seen her. Pam was punching Lesley in the back. It hurt, but Lesley wanted her to carry on. Those bruises would be the very evidence she needed when she went to report her and Nuri for cruelty. Pam carried on shouting all the usual rubbish she always shouted. Ungrateful bitch, you deserve to be in the work-house, slut, Lesley had heard it so many times she could have shouted at herself!

Pam dug her talons into Lesley's arm. 'If I hear you have been in town again, you will be in serious trouble. Do you understand me?'

Lesley nodded, thinking that she and Margo would have to go somewhere if Lesley was to have any hope of stopping the cruelty. Pam stormed out and Lesley dearly wanted to throw her hairbrush at the door, but she didn't dare. Instead she punched her pillow really hard, imagining each punch was Pam's face.

The next day, Lesley told Margo what had happened and as always Margo listened to her tale of woe. She could not understand how anyone could have such vile parents. They had adopted Lesley; why adopt a child then treat it like this?

Once again, Margo took Lesley home to her house. She asked Lesley to show her mum the bruises that were now a lovely shade of purple on Lesley's back. Lesley was petrified of what the consequences would be should she be seen leaving school again.

'Oh dear,' Margo's mum said. 'Those are some rare bruises, aren't they? It just so happens I have found someone who will help you. He is an inspector for the NSPCC.'

Lesley had never heard of them. 'Who are they?' she asked.

'It's an organisation called the National Society for the Prevention of Cruelty to Children,' Margo's mum replied. 'I can't take you – you have to go yourself – but I'm sure Margo will go with you if you want some moral support.'

Lesley thought she would need all the support she could get. Here was a chance of help, but Lesley was shaking with fear at the thought of having to explain what was happening in her life and what had been happening for the last eleven years. She would be sixteen in the August of 1974 and desperately hoped to be away from that horrid house in Jerviston Street by then. Even if she had to go to a children's home, it would be better than living in that house with those horrible people and their brats. The girls rushed back to school in time for registration and made a pact that they would go to the YMCA office in Motherwell, where the man was based, the following lunchtime.

The next day at school, Lesley couldn't concentrate on her lessons. She and Margo messed about in the French lesson and were reprimanded by the teacher. They just laughed. They sat at the back of the class with Janice, Joyce and Lorna, giggling and chattering till the teacher was very cross. They tried to be good but all they could think about was the visit they were going to make at lunchtime. Lesley was excited, but she was terrified of what would happen when these people contacted Pam and Nuri. Would that be the very last straw that meant they would actually kill her? Her mind was in turmoil.

At lunchtime, the two girls made their way to the YMCA office in Brandon Parade. It was a beautiful old building, but Lesley didn't really take much notice as she and Margo climbed the stairs to the NSPCC office on the first floor. Margo knocked on the door, as Lesley's hands were shaking so badly she couldn't manage it.

A gentleman opened the door to the girls. He was very smartly dressed in a tweed suit, he wore pince-nez glasses which the girls found amusing and he had grey hair which had gone white in places. He was very softly spoken and Lesley trusted him, sure she could tell him everything without being judged.

'Can I help you?' he asked.

Lesley took a deep breath. She wasn't sure whether she wanted to go through with this, or whether she should run away and spare herself another beating. She decided getting help would be the most sensible option. She started to speak. 'It's me that needs help, sir,' she said. 'I don't want to waste your time, sir, but ...' Lesley's voice trailed off, terror gripping her heart as she realised that now there was no going back.

The man smiled kindly. He had heard it so many times before and this girl looked so afraid, he took pity on her. 'I'm sure you wouldn't have come if you didn't need my help. Now then, what seems to be the problem?'

Lesley tried to explain, but the words were tumbling out of her mouth so fast that she found herself getting everything jumbled up.

Luckily, Margo interrupted and said, 'Show him. Show him your back.'

Lesley removed her school blazer and slowly lifted her jumper to reveal the bruises on her back, which were slowly turning fifty shades of purple and green. The man

166

looked at the bruises and the other scars on her back. *Obviously this is not the first beating,* he thought. 'How old are these bruises?' he asked Lesley.

'Yesterday, sir.'

The man put a calming hand on Lesley's shoulder. 'It's alright, dear. You really mustn't be afraid of me. I am here to help you.'

Lesley could feel the tears welling up in her eyes. At last, somebody believed her! The man instructed Lesley to stay still while he took photos of the bruises on her back. Lesley smiled inwardly. Now Pam couldn't deny that she had beaten her. 'Are those the only bruises?' the man asked.

Lesley was just about to say yes, when Margo piped up from the corner, 'Your arms. Show him your arms.' Lesley rolled up her shirtsleeve to reveal five perfect nail marks, some of which had broken the flesh on her arm.

'What did those?' the man asked her. 'Please, sir, the woman who adopted me, she did it. She has long nails and she has been digging them into my arms since I was four.' The man didn't much like the sound of this woman; she sounded like a delinquent.

Suddenly, the two girls were in a panic. 'We have to go sir. Lunchtime is nearly over. We can't be late.'

The man instructed the girls to return the following day, when he would take some more details and advise Lesley what she needed to do next. Lesley and Margo ran all the way back to school and arrived just in time for afternoon registration.

That night, Lesley once more avoided the stupid blue Transit camper sat the other side of the school and walked up the other way. She needed time to get her head around what might happen next in her pitiful, pointless life. The evening passed peacefully. Lesley remembered to remove the lunch ticket for that day so as to avoid another punch-bag session with Pam.

The next day, filled once more with excitement and trepidation, the two girls went to the NSPCC office.

The nice man let them in and sat them both down. 'Right then. Today we need to get a few details down, then I can set the wheels in motion to get this situation sorted,' he said. 'My name is Frank Kennerley and I am the area officer for the NSPCC. Here is my card, which you need to keep safe.'

Lesley started to shake again. It was all too real and she wasn't sure she had the courage to go through with this.

'Now, what is the telephone number where you live?' Mr. Kennerley asked.

'I can't give you that, sir,' Lesley said, wringing her hands. 'If you ring the house, they'll know I've been here and they'll kill me!'

Mr. Kennerley put a calming hand on Lesley's little hands, which were cold and clammy with the fear she felt. 'If they beat you, any time, no matter what for,' he said, 'you are to call me immediately. Is that clear? I also need you to keep a diary of when they hit you, punch you, beat you or anything else, for the next two weeks. Once I have some concrete dates and reasons for the beatings, I can progress the matter further.'

Lesley and Margo once more set off back to school, discussing their meeting with Mr. Kennerley on the way. Lesley felt a great sense of relief as she realised that Mr. Kennerley never once said she was a liar, never once said that she had made all this up. He believed her.

Lesley returned to her prison in Jerviston Street with a lighter heart that evening. She was confident that Pam and Nuri would not be able to resist the urge to beat her for something in the next few weeks, but, unlike the previous years of abuse, this time they would be signing their own fate.

A few days later, that Saturday, Lesley had been doing her jobs as usual. She dusted, she hoovered, she mucked out the dog shed in the garden, which reeked of urine and faeces. Lesley didn't see why she should be doing all these jobs. After all, Lucy and John were now old enough to help around the house, but they were never made to do anything.

She finished her chores and went up to her bedroom to start her homework. Pam and Nuri were in her bedroom. Lesley's heart sank. What would it be this time? The constant shouting and beatings were really annoying her now and she was counting the days to her sixteenth birthday, when she could walk out of the door and never return. Nuri ordered Lesley to sit down on the bed. He looked menacing, stood over her. 'How much money have you got?' he asked her.

Lesley almost wet herself. Had they found the money she had hidden underneath the bookshelf? The money that Uncle Roy had been sending her to buy herself a few bits? 'I think I have fifty pence,' she replied.

'Well,' Nuri continued, 'if that's the case, where did this come from?' In his hand he was holding a Max Factor talc which one of the girls at school had given her out of pity. Lesley was furious with them. While she was slaving, cleaning that horrible house for them and their brats, they were searching her room, again! Lesley longed for the day when she had her own room and nobody would search through it while she was out.

Lesley stood up. She decided that she would goad them, then they would beat her because they just couldn't help themselves. That would give her the ammunition to set the wheels in motion for them to get into big trouble with the authorities. 'All my friends are allowed perfumes, deodorant, makeup,' Lesley said defiantly. 'You barely pay me enough money to afford my sanitary towels. My friend gave me that talc because she felt sorry for me and the life I have to live.'

Nuri looked as if he might explode and disappear in a puff of smoke. 'You mean you told people we beat you?' he shouted.

Lesley felt triumphant now. She had hit the right nerve; this was going to kick off and she would sit and laugh when they were prosecuted by the NSPCC. As usual, the beating was dished out, but this time, because they were so angry, they had a field day, punching, kicking and hitting her with the riding crop wherever it landed.

Lesley stood up and laughed.

'What are you bloody laughing at?' Pam asked her.

'Nothing,' Lesley said. She sat on her bed and waited till they left the room before crying.

She could hear Pam on the landing. 'That girl's mad, just like her mother.'

Monday morning came around and Lesley resolved that she would go and see Mr. Kennerley at lunchtime. Margo couldn't go with her this time, so Lesley went alone. She ran all the way there, in case anyone saw her out of school again. Luckily, Mr. Kennerley was in his office when she arrived at the YMCA.

'Back so soon?' he asked her. 'I take it all is not well.'

Lesley looked at him. Without speaking, she rolled down her tights, revealing black and blue legs with bruising from top to bottom. She rolled up her shirt sleeves. Where the scratches were previously, there were now bruises and scratches on both arms. She pulled up her shirt and showed him the bruising on her back, more severe than the previous beating had produced.

Mr. Kennerley looked stern. He knew this child was not lying and he knew there was a serious problem in her household. 'When did this happen?' he asked her.

Lesley replied meekly, 'Yesterday.'

'May I ask why?' Mr. Kennerley couldn't wait to hear what lame excuse there would be for beating this child black and blue.

Lesley explained how they had searched her bedroom while she was doing their cleaning and they had found the talcum powder container she had hidden in her wardrobe. She told him how, even though she was nearly sixteen, she was not allowed perfume or talc or makeup like her friends were.

'Right,' said Mr. Kennerley. 'This ends now. I need the telephone number of where these monsters work, both of them. Let's get some photos of these bruises before they start to fade. I've had enough of this now.'

Lesley felt chronic fear. A cold terror was taking over her whole body and she feared that she would definitely be murdered now she had told tales. Lesley's mind was locked in a trance. Fright had completely enveloped her mind and she wasn't listening any more.

'Lesley,' Mr. Kennerley said. 'Are you listening to me?'

Lesley suddenly realised he had been speaking and she had not heard a word. 'I said, we will be sending a policeman to school to interview you. Your teachers will be told that they are not to contact Pam and Nuri at all, otherwise they will be prosecuted. Once the police have taken a statement from you, your case will be put forward for consideration by the Children's Panel, who will decide

how we can get you away from there and keep you safe.'
Lesley thought that she probably wouldn't live long
enough to be taken to safety, but right now, death was a
pretty safe option, so it didn't matter.

She turned to face Mr. Kennerley. 'Please sir, what will
happen to me? Will I have to go to the workhouse?'

Frank Kennerley was a wise man. He had been in this
job for many a year and seen many cases of cruelty pass
through his office, but he had never seen such terror in the
eyes of a child as he saw now in Lesley's eyes. She was
truly frightened of those people, and they must be stopped,
whatever it took. He cleared his throat. 'Excuse me, who
said anything about the workhouse?' he asked her.

Lesley once more explained that she was always being
threatened with the workhouse and being fed bread and
water.

'Believe me, you're not going to any workhouse, young
lady.' Mr. Kennerley was adamant he would do all he
could to help this child. 'Don't be frightened, Lesley,' he
said kindly. 'You've done nothing wrong. If they beat you
again they will be arrested, no questions asked. This kind
of cruelty is just not acceptable. Now, run along back to
school and I will arrange for a policeman to come and
interview you.'

Lesley could just imagine the looks on the children's faces
when a policeman appeared at school and hauled her out of
the class. They would think she had been shoplifting or
worse. She imagined the look on Pam's face when they went
to her place of work and hauled her out to be interviewed.
Lesley smiled as she thought of the fear that Pam would feel;
she deserved a taste of what she was dishing out.

She arrived back at school and joined the class for
registration. Margo asked her how she had got on and she

explained, in between being told off by the teacher for talking, that if they beat her again, they would be arrested. Margo found that quite funny. She didn't like Pam either. Margo was pleased that her friend was finally going to get a solution to her problem.

Chapter 13

Escape from Hell

❦

Lesley walked home even more slowly from school that evening, mulling over how events were turning out. She deliberately avoided the horrible pale blue Transit van parked at the other entrance to Dalziel High School in Hamilton Road. No way did she want to have anything to do with that woman any more, unless she had to. Lesley didn't know when the police were going to interview Pam and Nuri so she was very careful, watching for any change in their attitude or body language, but they were the same as usual. Lesley sat quietly at mealtimes. She had always wondered why they ever bothered to adopt her, but she wasn't about to ask them now. Maybe one day she would pluck up the courage and ask that question, but not now.

The next morning, Lesley went to school as usual. She talked to Margo about what they thought might happen when the police had been round to the house. Before she left the house, Lesley had checked her 'Leaving Here' chart. This was a grid she had in one of her exercise books – a bit risky, but it gave her pleasure to cross the days off. The chart said 137 days left in that house. It seemed like an eternity, but Lesley knew that she would be free by the end of the summer holidays in 1974.

Lessons started for the day. Just after the morning break, the school secretary came into her English lesson and asked if Lesley could be excused as the police wished to talk to her. The children started sniggering, but the few who knew what was going on wished her luck as she left the classroom.

Lesley was ushered into an empty classroom.

'Good afternoon, dear. My name is PC Williams. I have come to have a chat with you, but I don't want you to be frightened.' He beckoned Lesley to an empty chair in front of him. She sat down nervously. This was real now. It was really happening.

PC Williams asked Lesley some mundane questions. How was her exam revision going? Had she been enjoying the lesson he'd pulled her out of?

Lesley wasn't taking much notice. She gave 'yes' or 'no' replies as she thought appropriate. Her brain was in overdrive.

PC Williams then asked Lesley to start at the very beginning, from when she had arrived in Motherwell. He asked her to recall her very first memory and how she came to arrive at Pam and Nuri's house.

Lesley explained about how she had met Pam and how she had slapped her even before she had adopted her! She told him about the coach journey and how she hadn't realised where she was going till the coach was bound for Scotland.

PC Williams was a very kind man, with a young family of his own. He knew teenagers could be difficult, but he didn't feel that beating them would solve anything. In fact, it could just make things worse. He asked Lesley how many times she had been beaten since she was in Motherwell.

Lesley replied that beatings, slappings and punchings were a routine part of her daily life; she couldn't possibly quantify them. Lesley told him about the time she had her Christmas presents confiscated. She told him about Pam throwing all the lovely new things her grandparents bought her in Brighton into the dustbin. She told him how she had run away nine times because she was so miserable there, but every time she was forced back into that house.

PC Williams decided he didn't like these people. They sounded like monsters. He wrote everything down that Lesley told him, and he told her that he was now going to confront Pam, at Hamilton Academy, in front of everyone, about what she had done. He said that the humiliation of a policeman arriving to pull her out of a class would be a good starting point for the next course of action.

Lesley heard the bell go for the next lesson; she'd already missed two lessons and a break. 'I'd better go,' she said. 'My friends will think you arrested me and took me away.'

PC Williams smiled. 'All right, but let me tell you, you're not the one who will be arrested in this mess.'

Lesley smiled and dashed out of the classroom to her next lesson. She was now a nervous wreck. She was surely going to be beaten black and blue tonight, after the police had spoken to Pam.

Lunchtime came and she ran to Mr. Kennerley's office. He tried to calm her down, but Lesley was in no mood to calm down and she was terrified.

'I know I came to ask for your help,' she started, 'but I am so scared. I can't go home to that house tonight. They'll kill me! I know they will. This is all going too fast for me.' Lesley started sobbing. She was angry with herself for not being strong enough to just put up with the abuse till she could leave home.

Mr. Kennerley spoke kindly but very firmly. 'Now look, I know you're scared. That's perfectly normal. Their behaviour towards you has been unacceptable right from the start and they will be held to account. I assure you, if

176

they so much as lay one finger on you from now on, they will be arrested and sent to prison. You have nothing to fear any more. If it will make you feel better, I will ring the house tonight and make sure you are all right. How does that sound?'

Lesley felt just a little reassured by this promise, but she was still very afraid. She walked home from school, very, very slowly. What was the worst that could happen? Another beating with the riding crop? How she wished the thing would break so that they could never use it again. They might throw her out. No – she could never be that lucky.

By the time she reached the front gate, Lesley had a very slight spring in her step. She thought it best to sit tight and see what would happen next. The hideous blue Transit van was already on the drive, so she knew Pam was already home from school.

Lucy was at the back door. 'Oh boy, are you in trouble!' she said. Lucy was now nine years old, an obnoxious, precocious child. Lesley hated her, and John as well. They never got told off, they never got a beating, and they made stories up and told tales so that Lesley would get the beatings instead. She couldn't wait to get away from these brats.

Pam was sat at the kitchen table sobbing. Lesley was ecstatic to think that just for once, someone had made her cry instead of the other way round. She looked up at Lesley. 'I hope you're satisfied, you bitch.'

Lesley wanted to laugh at the self-pity exuded by this monster, but instead she calmly smiled and said, 'Serves you right.' Lesley carried on up to her bedroom. *How have the mighty fallen*, she thought to herself. *You're not so brave now, are you?*

Lesley heard Nuri come in. The sobbing got a bit louder, then there was shouting, then all went quiet. Lesley heard footsteps on the landing outside her door. She was quite prepared for a beating tonight.

Nuri came into her bedroom. He was carrying the riding crop in his hand. Lesley was ready for him. 'What's your game?' he asked her, almost spitting the words out.

Lesley looked at him. She wasn't afraid any more. She pointed to the riding crop. 'See this?' she sneered at him. 'If you so much as lay a finger on me or either of you touch me ever again, you'll go to prison.'

Nuri stood up. His expression was evil, but this time Lesley had the upper hand. He lifted his arm as if to slap her.

'Go on then! Hit me!' she goaded him. 'I can't wait to call the police and tell them. Then you'll be in big trouble!' Lesley was enjoying this. Now she had the upper hand. The bullies were not quite so brave any more.

The evening meal was eaten in complete silence. After they had eaten, Pam and Nuri disappeared into the lounge, no doubt trying to think of how they could lie their way out of their predicament.

Around 7 p.m., the doorbell rang. Lesley went to the door and there was Mr. Kennerley. 'Still alive, then?' he asked her with a grin on his face.

'So far,' Lesley chuckled. She showed him into the lounge and as she closed the door she wished him good luck. Mr. Kennerley had no idea how horrible these two could be. Lesley smirked as she thought of him showing them the photos of her terrible bruises and them trying to lie their way out of any blame. Even if they did try to lie, the photos were enough to bury them. Besides, Margo also knew what was going on and she had seen the bruises too.

Lesley went up to her bedroom and carried on with tidying her room and doing her homework. After about an hour, Nuri appeared at the door. 'Mr. Kennerley wishes to speak with you. Pam and I will be in the piano room,' he said. Lesley was pleased that they would be across the hall – they wouldn't be able to eavesdrop on the conversation.

Lesley went down to the lounge and Mr. Kennerley beckoned her to come and sit down. 'Well, that was a very interesting conversation,' he said. 'If those two thought they were going to get one over on me, they were wrong. They tried the sob-story routine first, then told me that you have always been a difficult child, badly behaved and hard to control. Of course, they denied everything, as we knew they would. They denied the beatings, until I produced photographic evidence. Then they tried to convince me that you put the bruises on your body all by yourself. For intelligent people, they are really rather stupid.'

Lesley felt vindicated. She knew now that she had done the right thing by seeking help.

'Anyway,' Mr. Kennerley continued, 'I have told them in no uncertain terms that any more violence of any kind towards you will result in them being prosecuted.'

Lesley was so pleased she wanted to dance round the room, but that didn't seem quite appropriate.

Mr. Kennerley continued, 'From now on, I will collect you on a Saturday and we will have a couple of hours out, away from the house. That will give you a fair chance to tell me anything that you feel I should know. If I am around, they won't be able to dish out any sneaky beatings. They'll know that you will tell and they will be in more trouble than they are already.'

Lesley was delighted. Her little body ached enough as it was.

Mr. Kennerley walked to the front door, assuring Lesley that he would be back on Saturday to take her out for a couple of hours. This was not negotiable, so any efforts on Pam or Nuri's part to stop her would be a very bad move. The younger children were always around, sneering, goading, trying to get Lesley to lose her temper with them. She did her very best to ignore them and shut them out of her life. They were not even related to her and she hated them.

After Lesley closed the front door, she thought about what might happen next. Would she get a beating? Would they throw her out tonight? She started to head for her bedroom but was called back by a red-faced Nuri.

'You've really done it now, haven't you?' he shouted at her. 'Fancy telling a complete stranger your whole life story and worse still, showing him your body! What are you thinking of, girl?'

Lesley found this quite amusing. They were more bothered about the fact that Mr. Kennerley had photos of her body than about the fact they were in big trouble for beating her! Lesley always thought they were a few sandwiches short of a picnic, but this was something else.

Pam picked up the reins now and carried on. 'Do you realise that if we hadn't taken you in, you would be in the workhouse, living on bread and water? You would have to scrub the toilet with a toothbrush.'

Lesley found that concept quite appealing, as opposed to being the slave for this household and being rewarded with endless beatings.

'What have you got to say for yourself, girl?' Pam bellowed.

Lesley thought for a moment. For years she had been too afraid to open her mouth. Now she had the police and

Mr. Kennerley on her side, she could say what she wanted and they couldn't lay a finger on her. Lesley took a deep breath, and then she began. 'I don't remember ever being asked if I wanted to come and live here. In fact, when you came to Reading,' she stopped to jab a finger at Pam, 'I seem to remember you slapping me when you put me to bed. I didn't know who you were or what you were doing in our house, but I didn't like you then and I don't like you now. After all the beatings I have had to endure over years, I quite fancy going to the workhouse. I bet I wouldn't have had half as many beatings there. Anyway, I'm sixteen in August and I can't wait to get away from here.' Lesley waited. She'd said her piece and now she braced herself for the fall out.

Pam and Nuri looked at each other. Pam spoke. 'I think you have made your feelings perfectly clear. If you want to leave, feel free. We don't want you here any more. You can go and live your free life in the gutter, breeding children like rats with no husband to help you. Feel free.' With that, they both left the room.

Lesley thought that if they could have given her a good beating, they would have, but now they didn't dare. She climbed the stairs, wary of any flying objects that might come her way from above or below, but all was quiet.

Lesley went about her chores with slightly less diligence. She knew they could no longer throw shoes at her, or tins of anything. They couldn't drag her round the house by her hair or destroy her bedroom, so that she would have to put it all back together again. Life didn't feel quite so bad now.

That was not quite the end of the matter. Every opportunity Pam got, she would jibe about how Lesley had to be out of the house by the day of her sixteenth birthday, otherwise she would be thrown out in the street. Lesley tried not to worry. She hoped that a miracle might happen and Mr. Kennerley might find her a nice home to go to. True to his word, every Saturday he would call at the house and take Lesley out for an ice cream or a cup of tea, maybe to New Lanark, where they could walk and Lesley could unburden herself of her worries without anyone listening. Lesley loved the waterfalls at New Lanark and the long walk that soothed her soul.

When it was time to return home in the evening, Mr. Kennerley noticed how Lesley would suddenly go quiet and retreat back into her shell. As they pulled up outside the house, he said, 'Do you know what? I am going to call this place Bleak House. It gives me a sense of foreboding and doom.'

Lesley laughed then; she knew exactly what he meant.

The falls of New Lanark, the peaceful haven where Frank Kennerley used to take Lesley to escape from Pam and Nuri on a Saturday.

Mr. Kennerley was talking to Lesley one day when they were out. He asked her where her sister was. Lesley explained that she didn't even know where the Isle of Man was and she didn't know where her sister was.

'Would you like me to find out for you?' he asked.

Lesley nodded. There was nothing she would like more than to know where her sister was. 'I will get her address for you,' he said. 'Someone in this godforsaken family must know where she is.'

As all this turmoil was going on, Auntie Golly came to stay with her grumpy parents down the road. She had a daughter, called Rachel. Rachel was an only child, very spoilt and very knowing. She had obviously heard the adults talking about what was going on in Jerviston Street and had realised that Lesley was adopted. She took great delight in telling Lucy and John about this. One day, when Lucy and John were being particularly difficult, Lesley told them to go and play on their own. They immediately started teasing her about the fact she was not their sister, and that Rachel had told them. Lesley didn't care. She hated the brats anyway; they were obnoxious, like their parents.

The 'Leaving Here' chart was still being ticked off, one day at a time. Now it was down to sixty days. Lesley was excited to think that she could escape from this house once and for all but a little apprehensive about whether she would actually have a roof over her head. Mr. Kennerley came to visit as he had been doing for a few months. Margo and Lesley got into a few scrapes at school together, but Lesley found it liberating. She had been a goody two shoes for too long and yearned to be counted amongst the badly behaved girls of the school.

One day, when they were out, Mr. Kennerley said he had

something to tell Lesley. She was a bit nervous about this. She sincerely hoped he wasn't going to say he'd left his job. Luckily for her, it was the best news she could have wished for. 'I've got you a job you're going to love,' Mr. Kennerley announced. 'It's working with children just like you who have been mistreated at home and have been taken into care. You'll be looking after them, getting them up for school, putting them to bed, helping with their homework, doing some food preparation and laundry to help out. There's a lovely bungalow separate to the home where you can live in your own fully furnished room. How does that sound? Don't tell Pam and Nuri yet though.'

Lesley was overcome with emotion. She wouldn't have to worry about going to the workhouse or sleeping on the streets any more. She would have a proper job, with a wage. It was all so exciting. She promised to keep her news quiet until Mr. Kennerley said it was all right.

The exams were coming up and Lesley revised hard, hoping to get the best grades she possibly could. Her dreams of going to university were still alive, so she did her best, knowing that the better her grades, the better choice there would be of jobs. She wanted to take the job Mr. Kennerley was offering, but she wanted to have a good set of exam results so that she could better herself in years to come. The exams were very hard. This wasn't helped by the fact that the invigilators were so strict that the pupils hardly dared look up from their exam papers. Lesley did her very best. The teachers said that if pupils could show how they had arrived at the answers they had given, they might be awarded more marks, even if the answer was incorrect.

After a few weeks, the results arrived. Lesley wanted to go and hide, hoping to open her envelope before Pam could see her results. She was not so lucky. As soon as the post arrived, Pam appeared from nowhere and snatched the envelope from under Lesley's nose. Pam opened the envelope, very slowly, as if to prolong the torture of not knowing what the results were. Lesley stood and waited while Pam read down the list of subjects and the marks next to them. Then she threw the exam certificate back at Lesley in disgust. 'You stupid bitch. Just as I thought, you'll never amount to anything. You are thick and stupid and the only life you'll have is in the gutter.'

Lesley nervously looked down at the paper she was holding in her hand. She had an 'A' in English, French and German. Her arithmetic score was a 'B', however she had failed the mathematics part of the exam, which consisted of algebra, geometry and trigonometry. Lesley wasn't too bothered; she had wanted to do well in her languages and at least she had passed the arithmetic part of the exam, which meant she could work in an office or even in a shop.

Just Lesley as was mulling over what options might be available to her, Pam started again. 'Well, guttersnipe, useless creature that you are, best you find somewhere to live as soon as you are sixteen. You certainly won't be staying here. Simon managed to do so well, he got into university and is now doing a master's degree. You, on the other hand, are far too stupid to achieve anything in your life.'

Lesley had, by now, reached a point where she didn't care what Pam said any more. Any emotion she felt was swept aside by the thought of being able to escape to the children's home and be rid of this monster forever. Lesley decided that she must speak to Mr. Kennerley. He had to get her out of there before her sixteenth birthday, otherwise she would be on the streets. Lesley wasn't sure that Pam would carry out this threat, but she couldn't trust her not to.

Lesley telephoned Mr. Kennerley at lunchtime, using a telephone box across the road from Dalziel High School. She explained about the exam results. He was bemused by Pam's response but not surprised. Nothing would ever be good enough where Lesley was concerned. He tried to calm her down, explaining that Dundonald Children's Home was happy to take her, so not to worry. He told Lesley not to tell Pam anything at this stage, in case she had a mad fit and decided to throw her out on the street there and then.

Lesley called at the Army careers office to ask about enrolling for a career in the army. The lady was very nice, but she advised Lesley that nobody could be considered for a career in any of the armed forces until they had attained the age of eighteen. Lesley didn't have two years to wait. She needed a job with accommodation, available the minute she left school! What if Mr. Kennerley's contact changed her mind and Lesley was left to sleep on the streets? She didn't much like that idea.

A week passed by and Lesley heard no more. Pam gloated over her failed exam results and took every opportunity to humiliate her in front of relatives and friends who visited the house. It also seemed that the younger children, Lucy and John, had been told that Lesley was definitely not their sister, which is why she would be leaving the house very soon. Lucy was a poisonous little brat and taunted Lesley quite often about the fact that she could no longer tell them what to do because she was not their sister. Lesley didn't mind, but the younger children took great delight into doing some mischief and blaming Lesley for it, so as not to get the blame. Lesley hated everything about being in that house and all she could think of was how she was going to get out of there without ever having to return.

One evening, Mr. Kennerley arrived unannounced. He later explained to Lesley that he had done this deliberately, to try and catch Pam and Nuri unawares. He spoke to Pam and Nuri for what seemed an eternity. Eventually Lesley was called into the room. Pam and Nuri looked less than impressed, but Mr. Kennerley was smiling, so Lesley knew it must be good news. 'I have some very good news for you, young lady,' he said. 'Your school year finishes on Friday the twenty-eighth of June. Over that weekend, you must pack up all your belongings and have them ready for me to collect, along with you, on Sunday the thirtieth of June. Your new job at Dundonald Children's Home will start on Monday the first of July. You will have your own room in the staff bungalow, which you will share with two other girls.'

Lesley was really excited. It had finally been confirmed, and she no longer needed to worry about being homeless or jobless. Pam didn't look pleased. Lesley thought that this must be because she had hoped she would have the pleasure of throwing Lesley out onto the streets, now she was being denied that final sadistic pleasure.

'What will my job entail, please?' Lesley asked Mr. Kennerley. 'You will be looking after children like yourself, children who have been beaten and abused, just like you.' Mr. Kennerley shot a glance at Pam and Nuri, who were squirming in their chairs, helpless. They could no longer deny their wrongdoing; the photos of the bruising had been their downfall. Lesley was excited. She was finally being given an escape route, away from this awful house and these horrid people. Better still, it was in Ayrshire, away from Motherwell. She would no longer have to dread bumping into them in the street.

Mr. Kennerley continued to rub salt into the wound.

'You will be allocated a small group of children. It will be your job to get them up in the mornings, put them to bed at night and help prepare meals and do laundry. In fact, all the things you do now but you will be paid a wage for your efforts.' Mr. Kennerley had a cheeky smile, which Lesley liked. He winked at her as he said the last part of that sentence, and she knew what he meant. After all her years of slaving after everyone in that house with no reward apart from the roof over her head, she would be free.

Lesley asked Mr. Kennerley to tell her about Dundonald, as she had never heard of this place. Mr. Kennerley explained that Dundonald was a very pretty village in Ayrshire. He said that the home was set off the road, up a private drive. Dundonald had a chip shop, a village shop and a tiny post office. 'There are two buses,' Mr. Kennerley carried on. 'One goes to Ayr, one goes to Kilmarnock.' Lesley thought this place sounded like heaven! 'On your days off, you can get on the bus and go to the cinema in Kilmarnock, or you can go shopping in Ayr,' Mr. Kennerley finished. 'Now, I must be going, but remember, you must make sure you have everything you need ready for me to pack into my van on the thirtieth of June.'

'I will. Don't worry,' Lesley called out as he reached the end of the drive. She would most certainly make sure everything was packed. She never wanted to return to this hell once she had escaped from it.

The 30th of June came around and Pam was being particularly difficult about what Lesley could or could not take. She was instructed to leave certain things behind and she wasn't allowed to take all her clothes. Lesley didn't care. She hated most of the clothes in her wardrobe. They were old-fashioned, too big or too small and Lesley wanted to buy the things she wanted, not the things she was told to wear.

Mr. Kennerley put Lesley's belongings into his little van. She didn't have much, considering she had lived with these people for eleven years. He closed the doors to the back of his van and opened the passenger door for Lesley to get in. She was relieved that she was finally being rescued from this place. She didn't even turn round to wave to Pam and Nuri as Mr. Kennerley drove away.

As the car reached the end of Jerviston Street, Lesley started to laugh.

'What's tickling you, young lady?' Mr. Kennerley asked her.

'I'm free! I'm free! I have escaped from Bleak House and I never have to go back! I am so happy!' Lesley felt as if she had been released from prison after serving a life sentence. She told Mr. Kennerley about all the times Pam had ransacked her bedroom and pulled her out of her bed, before stripping it to the bed frame. She told him about all the beatings she had been given before she went to him for help. She told him about the incident with the soiled underpants in the primary school.

Mr. Kennerley was pleased that this story was going to have a happy ending. He had not been able to save all the children who needed his help. He dreaded the thought of what might have happened if he had not been asked to help Lesley. He decided that maybe she would have been better looked after in the workhouse.

Mr. Kennerley drove out of Motherwell and headed out towards Ayr. It was on the coast, a pretty little town. There were fields with sheep and cattle and the occasional horse. Lesley thought how pretty it was, how nice to be in the country, away from Motherwell and, best of all, away from Pam and Nuri.

Eventually, Mr. Kennerley pulled off the main road,

following the signs for Dundonald. Lesley was enthralled with the beauty of the countryside around there and when he drove through the village she was impressed with how pretty the main street was.

Mr. Kennerley pulled off the main road onto a farm track. Lesley could see a big house ahead. It looked like a stately home, but this was Dundonald House, a children's home run by the NSPCC. Mr. Kennerley drove past the big house and further on up the farm track. There was a slight curve in the track, and as they rounded the curve Lesley saw the bungalow which would be her home. They pulled up outside and Lesley clambered out of the van to get a better look at her new surroundings. The bungalow was set facing the farmer's fields. From within the bungalow, a face appeared at the door. It was a young girl in her early twenties, with long dark hair. She introduced herself as Shirley. Lesley thought she seemed very nice. Shirley took her inside and showed her around the bungalow, whilst Mr. Kennerley went down to the big house to announce that the new girl had arrived.

Shirley took Lesley into the lounge. It was a big room with comfortable furniture and brightly coloured wallpaper. At the end of the room, facing the farmer's field, was a huge window, which took up most of the end wall. The window looked straight out across the fields, which were filled with crops, ready for harvesting.

'What do you think?' Shirley asked.

Lesley was speechless. This looked like heaven. It was peaceful, it was pretty and it was a far cry from the cold, unfriendly house in Motherwell that Lesley had been forced to call home.

'Come on,' Shirley said. 'I'll show you your bedroom.' She took Lesley down the corridor, where there were four doors. 'That's my room, that's Claire's room and this one is yours,' Shirley said. 'Claire is on her days off, so she is visiting her family in Glasgow this weekend, but she'll be back on Tuesday and you'll get to meet her then.' Lesley looked round her bedroom. It was lovely. It had bright but tasteful wallpaper on the walls. There was a modern wardrobe and dressing table like the one Lesley had seen in Margo's bedroom. Her bed had a pretty flowery blue bedspread and the bedside lamp matched perfectly. Lesley knew she would be happy here. The last door was the bathroom, which also had modern fittings in it, not like the ancient antique bathroom Lesley was used to in Jerviston Street.

Finally, Shirley completed the tour with an introduction to the kitchen. It turned out that there was a kitchen etiquette which had to be observed by the girls. 'We each have a cupboard where we keep our own food,' Shirley explained. She opened her cupboard to reveal packets of cereal, some biscuits and a few tins. 'Same in the fridge. We each have one shelf, so that we don't get our food mixed up,' Shirley said. Lesley was happy with that. Nothing in Bleak House was ever hers exclusively, this was going to be a whole new experience.

Mr. Kennerley had arrived back at the bungalow in the meantime, bearing a set of keys for the bungalow's front and back doors, which he gave to Lesley. She couldn't believe her luck. Not only did she now have a lovely place to live but she had her own keys. Lesley was thrilled.

'Come on, then,' Mr. Kennerley said. 'We need to get your things out of my van into your room.' They unloaded the van, which didn't take long. Lesley didn't have much to call her own, despite living in Bleak House for eleven years. She didn't mind; she was free from her prison and, best of all, she was free of Pam and Nuri, forever.

Once everything was in her room, Lesley decided she could unpack later, so she asked if she could go to the big house for a look around. The house was on two floors. It was very long and Lesley wondered how many rooms there could possibly be in such a big place. Mr. Kennerley took her to meet the houseparents. They were in an office in one corner of the building.

A slim woman with a white apron on was sitting at one desk. She stood up and smiled as she came forward to greet Lesley. 'Welcome to Dundonald House,' she said. 'My name is Wendy and I am the housemother here. I trust you like your accommodation?'

Lesley smiled. 'Oh yes, thank you. It's lovely, not like the house I have come from,' she said excitedly.

'I have heard it wasn't very nice there,' Wendy said. 'Mr. Kennerley showed us the photos of your bruises. We've not seen cruelty like that for a while, I have to say. Still, there won't be any beatings here. I hope you'll be happy with us.'

Lesley nodded. Anywhere was better than where she had come from.

The man at the other desk had been on the telephone but now he came towards Lesley, shaking her hand firmly. 'I'm Duncan,' he said. 'I'm Wendy's husband and I am the housefather here.' Lesley thought she would be very happy here; everyone seemed so nice. Wendy offered to take Lesley on a tour of the building. Mr. Kennerley said his goodbyes and promised to return the following week to see how Lesley was doing.

Lesley followed Wendy up to the top floor. Wendy explained that boys and girls were kept separate, so Lesley must always make sure the interconnecting doors were closed or locked as she left each dormitory. There were about twelve to fifteen beds in each room, interspersed with wardrobes and chests of drawers. All the beds were neatly made, with brightly coloured bedcovers. Each dormitory had two bathrooms. Wendy explained that Lesley's duties would be to get the children up and make sure they went down for breakfast. Once they went to school, she must make their beds and clean the bathrooms. When she was finished, she was to go and either help Cook with preparation or the washing up, or she must help out in the laundry, doing washing and ironing.

Wendy carried on round the big house, showing Lesley each dormitory and explaining which age group lived in that particular room. It all seemed very straightforward.

Lesley returned to the bungalow and used her key to open the door. It felt warm and welcoming. She felt safe here. No more beatings. No more being blamed for Lucy and John's misdemeanours. No more being sexually assaulted by that vile Simon thing. Lesley went into the lounge and sat gazing across the fields. This was bliss. She had no money – Pam had made sure she wouldn't have anything to spend as her sick way of trying to humiliate Lesley – but for now it didn't matter. Lesley would be paid at the end of the week, then she could buy anything she wanted. Wendy said she could have something to eat in the big house, as part of her break during her eight-hour shift. Lesley was happy with that; she was used to not being fed.

She wandered outside and walked back down the track that led out of the home. It was a beautiful sunny day, so Lesley thought she would go into the village and have a wander round. After taking a couple of wrong turns, she found herself in the main street of Dundonald. It was a very pretty village, with neatly trimmed hedgerows and tidy little cottages on either side of the street. Lesley thought how novel, and how nice, it was not to have to ask permission to go out on her own. She had a little walk round, then headed back up to the bungalow. Once all her things were unpacked, she arranged her little ornaments in her room as she wanted them. Safe in the knowledge that what she put out would not be thrown on the floor to be tidied time and time again, she deliberately left her book on the floor and her nightie on top of her pillow, instead of underneath, as if in an act of defiance towards Pam.

Chapter 14

Freedom

———•❦•———

There was a part of her that was still afraid that they might come and fetch her back to Motherwell, but Lesley knew that Wendy and Duncan would not allow that. They were only too aware of the hell she had gone through in that house.

The first few days in her new job were a steep learning curve for Lesley. Although she had previously used a cooker and a washing machine, the ones in Motherwell had been old-fashioned. Dundonald Children's Home had all the latest gadgets, which took some getting used to. The staff were all very patient and helped Lesley as much as they could with her chores. They knew that she had not had an easy time in Motherwell, so they all went out of their way to make her feel safe and secure in her new environment.

Lesley loved being with the children. They were nice children, not like the spoilt brats in Bleak House. These children wanted someone to be nice to them; they were more than happy to play or to have some help with their homework. Lesley looked at the younger children and thought of herself at that age. She wondered how anyone could beat such a small child. Lesley wondered if she would ever be able to shrug off the fear she felt around older people.

Payday arrived and Lesley set off on the bus to Kilmarnock. After a good look around all the shops, she bought herself some makeup and a nice-smelling deodorant. Lesley could just picture Pam's face if she saw her now. There was a fashionable clothes shop in Kilmarnock with modern clothes in the window. Lesley went inside for a look round, no longer afraid to look at short skirts and low necked tops. She emerged from the shop, proudly carrying a navy blue mini skirt and a top to match. She felt very grown-up now.

Next Lesley spotted a café. She went inside and sat down. Now she could order her own food without having to ask permission. She ordered fish and chips, with a glass of Coca-Cola. Once she had finished her meal, Lesley headed back to get the bus back to Dundonald. Now she really felt like a new person. She was grown-up, she was free from her abusers and she was working. Lesley was looking forward to her future.

Afterword

---※◦⊙◦※---

Now you have read my story, I hope you have a clearer understanding of the life I had with my adopters. The people who were meant to give me a better life gave me a childhood I can only describe as a living hell. In fact, they took my childhood from me and I live with that every day of my life.

There is much more to tell. Abuse does not necessarily stop when you move away from your original abusers. Emotional and physical abuse were replaced by emotional and sexual abuse until I reached eighteen. That's another story which I will write. It will give you an understanding of how men find it easy and excusable to prey on vulnerable children. As an adult, men have treated me the same way. As soon as you admit you were abused as a child, a switch goes on and they think they can abuse you without guilt.

I have had counselling more than once. I have been prescribed medication more than once. The only healer for me has been to know that my abusers are now dead, that they can no longer frighten me or hurt me. I have revisited the house where the abuse took place in Jerviston Street. It feels totally different. The current owners are lovely and the house looks and feels like a warm, loving home. I arrived there in tears but left feeling happy and free – free of the demons that have haunted me for years.

I now have the inner peace I have been searching for since I left there in 1974.